The Graduate
Handbook

Dear Vonnie,

Congrats on a job well done!
May you greatly enjoy & be stretched
to seek Jesus more fully
while you are at CCU.

Blessings to you,
The Szymczak
Family

The Graduate
Handbook

Life Principles to Discovering Your Purpose,
Keeping Your Faith, and Preparing for What's Next

Jeffrey Dean & Robby McGee

 WordView

THE GRADUATE HANDBOOK
PUBLISHED BY WORDVIEW
1233 Northgate Business Parkway, Madison TN 37115

Details in some anecdotes and stories have been changed to protect the identities of the persons involved.

ISBN: 978-0-9887794-0-2

Published in the United States by WordView, Madison, TN 2013

Library Of Congress Control Number: 2012956052
Dean, Jeffrey; McGee, Robby
        The Graduate Handbook : Discovering Your Purpose, Keeping Your Faith, and Preparing for What's Next / by Jeffrey Dean and Robby McGee. – 1ˢᵗ ed.

Table of Contents

Start Here

"What are you going to do after you graduate?" That's the question you most often get asked when you're nearing high school graduation—right?

And most people think "I don't know" is the wrong answer to that question. As if there's something wrong with you if, at the age of seventeen or eighteen, you're not dead certain that you're going to start the next Apple…or head off to Mozambique with the Peace Corps… or enroll at Arizona State to study cactus biology.

Well, we don't agree. It's okay not to *know* what you're going to do after graduation.

But it's *not* okay not to *plan*!

You've got all kinds of decisions ahead of you, and you're going to be way better off if you are following a plan.

Once, while Jeffrey was speaking at the University of Kansas, he got to know a sophomore named Casey. Casey grew up in a Christian home in another city, became a Christian himself at a young age, and was active in church along with his family. Casey admitted to Jeffrey, however, that he had attended church only a few times since enrolling at KU.

"Why?" Jeffrey asked. "Is it that you're no longer interested in God?"

"Oh, no," Casey said. "God is still important to me." Then he thought about it for a minute. "I guess when

It's okay not to know what you're going to do after graduation. But it's not okay not to plan!

1

I came to college I just never really thought about going to church."

In other words, he hadn't *planned* it. And no plan usually equals no action.

That's just one small example of what we're talking about in this book. The same principle of needing to plan as you graduate from high school applies to *every* area of your life. Proverbs 21:5 (HCSB) says, "The plans of the diligent certainly lead to profit, but anyone who is reckless certainly becomes poor." God expects you to have a plan. Now, He doesn't expect you to rock it on your own. Look at Proverbs 16:9 (HCSB): "A man's heart plans his way, but the LORD determines his steps." He wants to be there every step of the way with you. But

He wants to be there every step of the way with you. But if you don't make any plans, what are you giving God to work with?

if you don't make any plans, what are you giving God to work with?

Having a plan prepares you not to give in to negative pressure in a moment of challenge. It also puts you in the right place to take advantage of opportunities as they come. What is your plan for the following areas?

- What will you do when your college roommate or friends engage in an activity with which you disagree?
- What kind of parties will you choose to attend or not to attend?
- What kind of person will you date?
- What will you do when a professor, friend, co-worker, or employer questions your faith?
- If you move to a new city, what kind of church will you look for?
- What steps are you taking now to prepare yourself financially for the future?

- Is it necessary for you to own one or more credit cards? If so, how many?
- When should you begin saving for retirement, and how can you get started?
- How can you choose the right career?
- How can you take steps each day to grow in your walk with God?

In the following chapters, we will offer answers to these questions— and many more—in an effort to help you develop a plan for your success.

Here's what we believe: *your planning releases God's direction*. Get used to that phrase, because you're going to see it again and again, in different forms, throughout this book in relation to the different topics of interest to high school grads that we cover. It's the key idea that will guide you through so much that you've got coming up over your horizon.

And that's why *The Graduate Handbook* isn't just another graduation gift to go along with the photo frame, college laundry bag, set of matching towels, or engraved coffee mug you received. (When will everyone learn the beauty and simplicity of these two words: *gift cards*!) This book is a must-read for the next stage of your life. We're a little biased, but we are confident that this book will be the all-encompassing, help-me-avoid-the-seemingly-unavoidable mistakes, set-my-sight-on-what-really-matters, get-me-through-the-big-issues-of-the-next-five-years-of-my-life book.

As your authors, we have a passion for helping guys and girls in their teens or early twenties get a great start on the life God wants for them. Jeffrey is a teen evangelist, author, and radio host. Robby is the CEO of an organization that funds international mission projects. Together, we bring over fifty years of ministry and business experience to the pages of this book.

The original inspiration for the book came after Tyler, Robby's son, had completed his first semester of college. While spending time at home during the Christmas break, Tyler began to share with his family some of his experiences from that first semester. Through hearing those stories, Robby quickly realized that, although he had tried to prepare Tyler for the post-high school launch, he had left a few crucial gaps.

A short time later, Robby shared Tyler's story with Jeffrey. We immediately joined our real-life ministry and business experience with our passion for working with young adults to provide you with the practical help and answers you will need during this time of your life. We grouped the information into topics, and one or the other of us individually addressed each of those topics in the chapters that lie ahead.

Our goal is to apply solid biblical truth, and the wisdom we've picked up along the way in our Christian lives, to the issues that concern you the most. Don't think you have to be a perfect Christian to benefit from this book (any more than Casey from KU was a perfect Christian). But if you're a follower of Jesus, or at least seeking to know Him, then we would ask you to be open to God's truth speaking to the real issues of your life. If you do that, we believe you'll avoid a lot of pain and get started on a life that's fulfilling to you and pleasing to God.

Our experience, however, tells us that those who read this handbook will fall into one of three categories:

1. The read-it, won't-accept-it, determined-to-ignore-it graduate
This graduate will read this book and choose to ignore these truths for life. It is almost certain that this graduate will make many of the mistakes discussed in this book in the next five years. Though this graduate will eventually realize the information in this book is true, he or she will continue repeating these mistakes throughout life.

2. The read-it, forget-it, regret-it, come-back-to-it graduate
This graduate will read the book and choose to walk away forgetting (or ignoring) most of the information received. It is almost certain that this graduate will make many of the mistakes discussed in this book in the next five years. However,

he or she will eventually come back to these truths in an effort never to repeat these mistakes.

3. The read-it, get-it, believe-it, and live-it graduate

This graduate will read this book (many chapters more than once) and choose to implement the information received. It is almost certain that this graduate will bypass many headaches and heartbreaks.

What about you? Which kind of graduate will you be?

The good news is, you get to decide which graduate you will be! Proverbs 16:3 (NIV) says, "Commit to the LORD whatever you do, and your plans will succeed." We hope you will decide now to commit your post–high school plans to God. He made you, He has been at work in your life since day one of you, and He has so much more He wants to do with you! As you begin to work through this book, commit now to becoming the read-it, get-it, believe-it, and live-it graduate.

You may want to read the book cover to cover right away. Or you may want to peruse the chapter titles and, for now, just turn to the topic that interests you most. For example, if you aren't going to college, the "College Life" chapter may not be for you right now. But you might be interested in the chapter about successfully interviewing for a job. Also, be sure to check out the related website— www.thegraduatehandbook.com—for more resources.

This is a handbook—a book meant to be held onto for years and dipped into when you need answers. Keep it near at hand. Read it when you need it. Follow the advice it offers.

Get started now...

Two Foundational Truths

1. The Word is essential to success.

Every challenge, encouragement, and life application in this book points to God's Word. The Bible is absolute truth. Everything begins and ends here.

2. Planning is essential to success.

The great divide that often separates those who thrive from those who merely survive is planning. Being strategic and intentional in every area of your life puts you way ahead of the crowd. This handbook will prepare you for the rest of your life.

I've Graduated....Now What?

Jeffrey Dean

Congratulations! You did it. After twelve years of fall break, Thanksgiving break, teacher in-service breaks, Christmas break, spring break, and summer break, the big break is finally here! School isn't just out for the summer; it's out for good. Shake your principal's hand, move that tassel, do your dance, and pose for the camera. You are a graduate!

Take a moment and take it all in. You deserve it. You've just closed a chapter on some of the best moments in the book called *My Life*. What a ride it's been, huh? Can you believe graduation is finally here? In the past seventeen-plus years, some if not many of the following have happened to you:

> You rode your bike without training wheels for the first time.
> You spent the night away from home (and Mom and Dad) for the first time.
> You got your first A.
> You got your first F.
> You popped your first pimple.
> You had your first crush.
> You had your first date.
> You prayed to have your first *second* date.
> You went to your first prom.
> You scored your first touchdown.
> You scored your first kiss.
> You worked your first job.
> You got your first paycheck.
> You drove your first car.
> You got your first speeding ticket.

You sang your first solo in front of a packed house…and you killed it!

You've covered a lot of ground since your first day of school. You've made a lot of memories. You've experienced a lot of firsts. And now, a new *first* that's also about a *last*—high school graduation. Countless others have stood where you now are and thought, *Free at last, free at last, thank God Almighty, I am free at last!* And, just as quickly, countless others have stood where you are, only to realize that "Thank God I'm free" can easily turn into "What in the world just happened to me?!"

The few months following graduation from high school are a mix of emotions at best. I wish someone had taken the time to talk to me about post–high school life when I was your age. These can be some of the best times of your life, but they can be some of the most influential as well.

During the next five years, change will be inevitable in many areas of your life, such as moving away from home, attending and gradu- ating from college, choosing a career, choosing a spouse, developing lifelong relationships, starting a company, join- ing a new church, traveling abroad, liv- ing abroad, purchasing a house, buying a car, applying for a loan, and much more! The next five years of your life are critical years for you. During these years, big decisions that will affect the rest of your life and those closest to you will be yours for the making.

During these years, big decisions that will affect the rest of your life and those closest to you will be yours for the making.

Exciting? It should be. Overwhelm- ing? At times it will be. Thrilling? Hope- fully so! You stand at a threshold with two guarantees: One, you never have to go to high school again! Two, everything is going to change and change fast!

Remember, your role moving forward is to plan. God's is to direct. Your planning releases His direction.

You can't control the unknown or unexpected. But you can position yourself so that, when change does happen, you aren't taken off-guard. I want to offer you a heads-up on some of the big changes I experienced along the way to help you be prepared to best respond to the *what's next* of post-graduation.

FREEDOM—AND RESPONSIBILITY— REQUIRED

Within a few months of receiving my high school diploma, I had moved out of the house, out of the state, and into a dorm room and was living with a guy I didn't know on a college campus full of people I had never met before. And it didn't start out so well.

You see, while in high school, I had wanted to pierce my ear. Keep in mind that this was long before it became the norm, especially for a guy, to have his ear, nose, lip, chin, eyebrow, or any number of other odd places pierced. My dad was adamant that as long as I lived at home I'd better not put a hole in any of my body parts. So, as you have probably surmised by now, once I got to college, I pierced my ear. In fact, I did it the first week of school. To save money, I had the piercing done by someone I met down the hall in my dorm. My life, my ear, and my freedom, right?

One of the biggest misconceptions most any eighteen year old has is that being a legal adult makes him or her a mature adult. Actually, the only big difference between your seventeenth birthday and your eighteenth birthday is that, starting with your eighteenth birthday, you get to go to jail with the big people if you screw up. So in this light, I guess I should have paused to consider that allowing someone I barely knew to stick a needle through my skin in his dorm room probably wasn't the smartest move. Several nights later, after a $420 visit to the ER because of an infected ear, I found out the important principle that with freedom comes responsibility.

Actually, the only big difference between your seventeenth birthday and your eighteenth birthday is that, starting with your eighteenth birthday, you get to go to jail with the big people if you screw up.

Until now, you've had someone helping to set boundaries in your life and making many of the big decisions for you. Now it's your turn. Now more than ever you have the freedom and responsibility to make your own decisions and set your own boundaries. In short, from here on—every choice matters!

LIFE WILL NEVER BE THE SAME

Of course, there is no way to know for sure what is ahead for you in life. But you can be sure of this—life will never again be as it was while you were in high school. Whether this is good or bad depends on many of the choices you make, especially within the next twelve months of your life.

Many of these changes are obvious, such as a new campus, job, friends, bedroom, and more. And many, if not most, of these changes you probably welcome. One biggie is that, from now on, consequences from a poor choice can be much greater than ever before. Up until now, your parents have probably disciplined you in love to the best of their ability. Going forward, however, mistakes no longer simply mean that you are grounded or lose your driving privileges for a weekend. Mistakes can be extremely costly, such as getting expelled from college, being fired from a job, losing your income, being incarcerated, and more. In short, the world's system of discipline won't judge the same as Mom and Dad have in the past.

FRIENDS WILL SCATTER

Most if not all of your friends will go their different ways after graduation. Some will go to college, others will begin a career, others will join the armed forces, and others will get married.

In the years since I graduated high school, I have seen only two of my high school friends, and that was just a handful of times. I have very little information as to where those friends are now or what they are doing with their lives. I have no idea where the rest of my high school friends are.

I realize that my situation may not become yours. But the point is, the likelihood that you will no longer associate regularly with your high school friends after graduation is high.

YOUR BELIEFS WILL BE TESTED

"I will give you an F if you don't remove the Scripture references from your term paper!"

I heard those words from my English 101 professor when I was a first-semester freshman attending Belmont University, a Christian school. Yes, a Christian school. I don't remember everything I wrote in that paper, but I do remember that the grade I received for it would be 100 percent of my grade for that class. I also remember using Scripture references several times throughout the paper to support my thesis. Thus my professor's startling comment.

My professor was adamant that God's Word was not relevant and reliable and had no validity in her class whatsoever. I knew my beliefs would be tested at some point during my collegiate experience. I never fathomed it would come this soon, not to mention from my professor at a Christian institution. I absolutely did not want to begin my collegiate career with an F. I also knew that I would be disappointed in myself if I didn't write what I believed in that paper and stand by it.

I chose to keep the Scriptures in the paper.

My professor didn't flunk me, but she did give me a D. It was the first D I'd ever made. I wish I could tell you that was the only D that I received throughout college. Unfortunately I cannot! But it *is* the one I'm most proud of.

Get ready! You're in for a similar ride. Your beliefs may not align with mine as it relates to God. But know this: your beliefs will be tested, whatever they are! This happened to me, and not just in English 101. By the time I finished my freshman year of college, my beliefs about God, heaven, and hell came into question from new friends and co-workers that I made and met. And it wasn't just my *spiritual* beliefs that were questioned. Likewise, there is a high probability that your beliefs about abortion, homosexuality, bisexuality, drinking, euthanasia, divorce, politics, the death penalty, and more will come into question in one way or another during the first few years after high school. This happened to me and it will happen to you too.

Do you know what you believe and why you believe it? Have you ever stopped to consider how, if asked, you would answer such questions as the following ones?

- What happens in the afterlife?
- Is it okay to marry someone of a different faith?
- Is abortion ever okay? Why or why not?
- What does the Bible say about homosexuality?
- If God loves everyone, why does He condemn people to hell?

This is just an example of what is to come. Now more than at any previous time in your life, it is critical that you know what you believe and why you believe it. Up until this point in your life, you have likely been surrounded and influenced by people with many, if not most, of the same beliefs as you. You, your parents, your family members, and current friends probably view things in a similar manner. This will change. Most of your new friends and acquaintances will have a different set of values than you and your family. If you aren't solid in what you believe and why you believe it, you will begin shifting in your beliefs, and eventually you will become someone very different from the person you are today.

The point I want you to grab here is that your beliefs will be challenged, and challenged often, in a variety of ways from a mix of people. One goal of this book is to help you fully develop your belief system and lay down a strategy for remaining aligned in God's Word so that you are prepared for the challenges of the next five years and the rest of your life.

ACCOUNTABILITY IS CRITICAL

Several people in my life today hold me accountable to God's truths. These are a variety of people—some are family members and some are friends, some are similar in age to me and some are older. Helping me manage my time, pushing me to reach my potential, calling me out when I appear to be straying spiritually, and praying with me and for me are just a few of the ways that some of the closest people in my life help to keep me accountable. Such a process isn't always comfortable or easy for me or them. However, these people are invaluable to me. And I hope I am the same for them.

I wish I'd had such people in my life when I was your age. I wish someone had told me the importance of having accountability partners and mentors in my life. I can't stress enough how critical it is that you surround yourself with people who will keep you accountable. Here the quantity of people is not as important as the quality. This role cannot simply be filled by close friends or peers doing what they normally do. I am talking about the kind of accountability

If you aren't solid in what you believe and why you believe it, you will begin shifting in your beliefs, and eventually you will become someone very different from the person you are today.

that isn't satisfied with yes or no answers—accountability that goes beyond "I'm doing fine" answers, accountability that will look you eyeball to eyeball and ask you the tough questions about your life.

Such counsel may not be easy to find. But I am confident that if you search for it, you will find it.

Four Truths About Counsel

1. Not all counsel is godly.

Proverbs 30:5-6 (NIV) says, "Every word of God is flawless; he is a shield to those who take refuge in him. Do not add to his words or he will rebuke you and prove you a liar." Sometimes even those with the best of intentions can mislead you by misquoting or mistaking what the Bible says. I learned quickly in college that there will almost always be a peer, professor, or co-worker who claims allegiance to God but offers counsel contrary to that claim. As you receive counsel from others, always use Scripture as the gauge by which you test such counsel to determine whether it is of God or humans. Simply put, if a person's suggestions, recommendations, or condemnations aren't in sync with God's, then such counsel is wrong, no matter how popular, culturally relevant, or accepted the person!

2. Not all counsel needs receiving.

You can't always control the counsel you hear, but you can control the counsel you choose to take in and act upon. Pray that God will guard your heart from hearing, receiving, and retaining ungodly counsel. Proverbs 1:5 (NIV) says, "Let the wise listen and add to their learning, and let the discerning get guidance."

3. Some counsel will require humility.

There is a myth that once you graduate from high school you suddenly have more knowledge. The key word here is *myth*.

Yes, hopefully the fact that you are graduating means that you have gained knowledge. But graduating doesn't mean you have gained all knowledge! The older I get, the more I seem to meet people who have more life experience, more wisdom, and more discernment than I. And though their counsel has often left me humbled, it has also brought to my attention areas of my life that need addressing while equally pushing me to be a better person.

4. Godly counsel is second to God's counsel.
"You guide me with your counsel, and afterward you will take me into your glory." The writer of Psalm 73:24 (NIV) understood that no counsel was more real and relevant for him than God's. Likewise, God desires a real relationship with you. Later in this handbook, I will talk in greater detail about steps you can take every day to know Him more. But know this now: if you commit daily to spending time with God, His counsel will guide you and grow you in ways far beyond your post–high school aspirations and dreams.

LIFT IT UP

Throughout this handbook, Robby and I will provide prayers to help you stop, think over what you have read, and pray it through. Obviously, you don't have to pray our written prayers word for word. But whether it's the words in this book leading you or your own, I hope you'll take the time to pause, reflect, and lift your heart to Him.

That is certainly something you should be doing as you look ahead to all the changes you can expect in the months and years ahead of you. You're about to make some big decisions that will help to set your course for life. So pray to God about it now.

Dear God,

Thank You for having Your hand on my life thus far. Thank You for bringing me to this new season of my life called post-grad. It would be foolish of me to believe I know it all and thus have no need to know You more. I want to know You more. I want to become the person You already know I can be. Throughout the next five-plus years of my life, I know there will be a lot to take in and live out. I don't dare go it alone. Please lead me. As I spend time in this handbook, show me what I need to see about myself. Show me areas of my life that need addressing. And prepare me to go and live the life You have created me to live as a Christ-follower honoring You in it all. Amen.

Chapter 2

What Do I Believe About God?

Jeffrey Dean

I remember many things about my senior year of high school. I remember the excitement of finally being a senior. I remember ACT and SAT testing. I remember flipping burgers at a local hamburger restaurant where I worked in our town. I remember wanting to date Stephanie. (Unfortunately, I also remember Stephanie never wanting to date me.) I remember all the fun Louis, my best friend, and I had on weekends. I remember singing solos at church. I remember wondering why I couldn't grow peach fuzz on my face even after going a full week without shaving. I remember the day I finally drove my restored '66 Ford Mustang to school for the first time. (It took me over a year from the time my dad and I bought it until I finally got it running.) I remember having to get my car towed home after school, on the first day I drove it to school, because it wouldn't start.

What will you remember most about your senior year?

Of course, if you haven't graduated yet, there is no way of fully knowing the answer to this question today. But be sure of this: you are making memories right now that you will cherish for a lifetime. And these experiences all contribute to your identity.

You see, your family, church, relationships, the culture, and more have all played important roles in shaping your values and beliefs—probably far greater roles than you realize. These values and beliefs are not only the core of who you are today but will also have a tremendous effect on what you believe and ultimately who you become throughout the rest of your life.

Up to this point in your life, you have had many voices speaking into your belief system—Mom, Dad, grandparents, friends, pastors, teachers, coaches, and more. It's probably safe to say that much of what you believe is a result of what you have been taught and expected to believe. It is also safe to say that once you graduate and move into new circles of influence, much of what you believe will be challenged by many new voices.

While speaking on a college campus recently, I met Kristin. She was in her sophomore year of college. She told me that she had gone through a "spiritual shift," as she called it, since graduating from high school. Kristin said, "I was the girl back home who grew up in church, attended all of the youth group events, went on several mission trips, and even consistently sang in the youth worship band." She then explained that since arriving at college, things had changed.

She told me what many college students often admit to me post–high school. "Once I got here and started making friends, I realized my beliefs about God weren't as strong as I thought. Church became less of a priority and sleeping in on Sunday mornings became routine."

Kristin went on to say, "By the end of my freshman year, I wasn't even going to church or really even reading my Bible. I admit that a few friends (and one professor in particular) have really pushed me to question a lot about my faith. I'm not sure where I am with it all right now. I guess you could say that I've lost confidence in some of the things I once believed about God and I'm still trying to figure it all out."

It is critical that you have confidence in what you believe. If you are not confident in what you believe and why you believe it, eventually your belief system will be shaken by someone, something, or some circumstance.

It is critical that you have confidence in what you believe. If you are not confident in what you believe and why you believe it, eventually your belief system will be shaken by someone, something, or some circumstance.

That's not to say that your beliefs should never change. The fact is, each of us is wrong about some things. After all, we are all human. And if you have been taught wrong, you believe wrong. If you believe wrong, you eventually do wrong. And if you do wrong, you will reap the consequences of doing wrong even if you think you are right.

In this chapter and the next, I want to focus on two big areas where it is critical for you to get it right. In Chapter 3 we'll look at the important relationships in your life, including family, friend, and dating relationships. Here in this chapter, though, we'll look at the most important relationship of all: your relationship with God. What religion is telling the truth about God—is it Christianity or some other religion? Where and how will you get better connected with God through a church?

The answers to such questions may not come easily. Even if you think you know the answers now, as your

After all, we are all human. And if you have been taught wrong, you believe wrong. If you believe wrong, you eventually do wrong. And if you do wrong, you will reap the consequences of doing wrong even if you think you are right.

transition from childhood to adulthood continues over the next few years, you will be challenged and influenced by a culture that has become increasingly secular, relative, and often discriminatory toward religion, in particular Christianity. Therefore, it is imperative that you not only *know* and find confidence in what you believe about God but also know what God *desires* you to believe. And as you seek to become more prepared for life in this area, God will guide you into truth.

Look, let me get personal with you for a moment. I am more confident today than ever before in my life of this:

I live as I believe.
I commit my life to those things in which I believe.
I will become what I commit my life to.

In short, if I believe what is right (God's truths) and commit my life to those beliefs, I will become the person He created me to be. If I believe something other than God's truths, no matter how much I believe I am right, I will be wrong and thus become the opposite of who He created me to be.

This stuff is important.

WHAT DO I BELIEVE ABOUT RELIGION?

Polling shows that 75 percent or more of the U.S. population believe in God, believe that the Bible is the actual or inspired Word of God, and consider religion to be important to them.

I live as I believe. I commit my life to those things in which I believe. I will become what I commit my life to.

Yet only 30 percent attend church on a weekly basis and only 16 percent read the Bible daily. Obviously, there is a huge disconnect between what people say they believe and how they actually live when it comes to the topic of religion.

This makes me think of what Jesus said in Matthew 7:21 (NIV): "Not everyone who says to me, 'Lord, Lord,' will enter the kingdom of heaven, but only he who does the will of my Father who is in heaven." Saying all the correct religious things isn't what grants us access to God and, eventually, to heaven.

What does your life prove that you really believe? Are you building your life on the solid foundation of Jesus's teachings or on the shifting sands of false beliefs (Matthew 7:24-27)?

You *can* know what to believe and how to live. Remember Foundational Principle 1 from "Start Here": *The Word is essential to success.* The Bible is absolute truth. It's how God teaches us what we need to know to live lives that are pleasing to Him. So let me give you some questions to answer concerning what you believe about religion. Then I will point you to the truth of Scripture to help you solidify what you believe.

1. Do I believe the Bible is the absolute truth of God?

Man does not live on bread alone but on every word that comes from the mouth of the LORD. (Deuteronomy 8:3, NIV)

As for God, his way is perfect; the word of the LORD is flawless. He is a shield for all who take refuge in him. (2 Samuel 22:31, NIV)

The entirety of Your word is truth, and all Your righteous judgments endure forever. (Psalm 119:160, HCSB)

Everything begins here. If you don't believe the Bible is the infallible Word of God, then it's only a matter of time before you lose confidence in who God is and His ability to guard and guide your life. You must know that you know that you know that the Bible is the infallible Word of God. Sure, just by saying this doesn't mean that you are confident in what you say. But this is the starting point.

Of course, the more you are in the Word, the more you will believe in the

If you don't believe the Bible is the infallible Word of God, then it's only a matter of time before you lose confidence in who God is and His ability to guard and guide your life.

Word. I'll give you some good advice in Chapter 10 about how to practically approach getting into the Word each day. But, for now, be confident in knowing that the Bible isn't just a book of words. The Bible is absolutely the words of God!

2. Do I believe all religions are the same?

See to it that no one takes you captive through hollow and deceptive philosophy, which depends on human tradition and the basic principles of this world rather than on Christ. (Colossians 2:8, NIV)

All religions are *not* the same. Some religious groups worship false gods. Some believe in God but don't believe that Jesus was His Son. Some believe Jesus was a real person but don't accept the fact that He died for us on the cross and was resurrected from the dead. Some don't believe the Bible is the infallible Word of God.

Christianity accepts God as the only God and believes that Jesus is the Son of God, who came to earth, died for humankind, and conquered death by coming back to life and proving that He is the one true Savior of the world. We believe the Bible is God's Word and the ultimate authority for everything we do. To be a Christian means one is a follower of Christ.

So before you believe the modern cliché that "all paths lead to God," do yourself a favor and consider what other religions are teaching in contradiction to the exclusive claims of Christ in Scripture.

3. Do I believe there are multiple ways to get to heaven?

Jesus told him, "I am the way, the truth, and the life. No one comes to the Father except through Me." (John 14:6, HCSB)

Christianity is based on a person's willingness to believe in and choose to live for Jesus. So Christians believe that faith in Jesus is the only way to get to heaven. You can't just be a "good person" or just do "good deeds" (though, of course, if you believe in Jesus, you will want to do those things). There's only one path to eternal life, and it's through Jesus.

How to Have a Personal Relationship with Jesus

1. Recognize God's plan.

God loves you and has a plan for your life. The Bible says, "God so loved the world that he gave his one and only Son, that whoever believes in him shall not perish but have eternal life" (John 3:16, NIV). This is God's plan for your life—that you spend an eternity with Him in heaven.

2. Realize the problem.

Every human chooses to disobey God and do his or her own thing. The result is that we are separated from God because He is perfect and we are sinners. The Bible says, "All have sinned and fall short of the glory of God" (Romans 3:23, NIV).

3. Respond to God's remedy.

Because God loves you so much, He sent His Son to bridge the gap between you and Him that exists because of your wrong choices. God's Son, Jesus Christ, paid the penalty for your sins when He died on the cross and rose from the grave. The Bible says, "God demonstrates his own love for us in this: While we were still sinners, Christ died for us" (Romans 5:8, NIV).

4. Receive Christ.

By asking Christ to come into your life, you cross the bridge into God's family. God then forgives you and offers you a relationship with Him and the privilege of spending eternity with Him in heaven one day. This is the *only* way to heaven! The Bible says, "To all who received him, to those who believed in his name, he gave the right to become children of God" (John 1:12, NIV).

Have you taken these steps to receive Jesus Christ as your personal Savior? These steps are far greater and more meaningful than any of those steps you will take to get up out of your chair, walk across that stage, and receive your high school diploma…and you don't have to wear a black gown and cap to receive it! You can stop right now, wherever you are, and pray a prayer such as this one:

Dear Jesus,
I realize that I am a sinner and I need Your forgiveness. I believe that You are the Son of God and that You died for me. I want to give my life over to You by asking You to forgive me of all my past mistakes. I now invite You into my life to save me and change me and be the Lord of my life. Thank You for loving me. Amen.

4. Do I believe that all other religions are false?

Watch out for false teachers. They come to you dressed as if they were sheep. On the inside they are hungry wolves. (Matthew 7:15, NLV)

As I just discussed in the last two questions, not all religions are the same, and there is only one way to God—through a relationship with Jesus Christ! I get it that it is not politically correct to say that there is only one true God and that His Son, Jesus, is the only way to Him. But I'm not writing this in an effort to help you remain politically correct. If you do not settle in your heart that all other religions are false, you will find yourself accepting them as equal and eventually fall into the deception of false teaching. If you don't believe all other religions are false, you will develop the "I'll consider your religion, if you consider mine" philosophy. Once you open up your mind to false teaching and being unequally yoked with someone of another religion (whether it be a friend, girlfriend, boyfriend, or spouse), you open yourself up to a spirit of deception.

5. Do I believe in the deity of Jesus?

In the beginning was the Word; and the Word was with God, and the Word was God. He was with God in the beginning.

All things were created through Him, and apart from Him not one thing was created that has been created. Life was in Him, and that life was the light of men. (John 1:1-4, HCSB)

The Bible is clear: Jesus is the Son of God. He was born of a virgin, lived a sinless life, was crucified, died for our sins, rose from the dead, and ascended to heaven to reign at the right hand of God.

Yet it will only be a matter of time before you will meet people who will try to convince you otherwise. It will only be a matter of time before you meet people who will tell you they believe in Jesus, only for you to discover that their religion actually believes that He was just a good man.

Of course, it is impossible for Jesus to have just been a good man. Many times, He made radical statements such as this one:

The one who believes in Me believes not in Me, but in Him who sent Me. And the one who sees Me sees Him who sent Me. I have come as a light into the world, so that everyone who believes in Me would not remain in darkness. If anyone hears My words and doesn't keep them, I do not judge him; for I did not come to judge the world but to save the world. The one who rejects Me and doesn't accept My sayings has this as his judge: the word I have spoken will judge him on the last day. For I have not spoken on My own, but the Father Himself who sent Me has given Me a command as to what I should say and what I should speak. I know that His command is eternal life. So the things that I speak, I speak just as the Father has told Me. (John 12:44-52, HCSB)

In these eight verses, Jesus claims that believing in Him is the equivalent of believing in God and that seeing Him is the same as seeing God. He said He is the light of the world and that He came to save the world. He goes on to say that anyone who doesn't believe in Him will be judged, that His words are God's words, and that they are everlasting!

If Jesus wasn't God, and wasn't the Savior of the world, and wasn't all He claimed, then the label *good man* wouldn't be fitting. Something more like—oh, I don't know—*liar, freak,* or *idiot* would be more fitting to someone who made such absurd claims!

WHAT DO I BELIEVE ABOUT CHURCH?

A friend of mine is a musician in Nashville. He moved to Nashville years ago to make it in the music industry as a session player. He has been there more than twelve years and has had a few opportunities to play in several bands and in a few recording sessions. But, as of yet, he hasn't had that big break into the industry that he desires. However, he does get to use his gift as a musician each week in his church. He's a really great drummer, and I love hearing him play during worship. He may never get that break he hopes for, but I know he knows that God is using Him to serve at his church each week.

Have you ever considered why you attend church?

People go to church for many reasons. Some attend out of a desire to know God better. Others attend church out of a sense of responsibility or guilt. Still others view church as a place to socialize or meet new people.

There are many reasons why you should go to church. The greatest of these is that you love God and desire to know Him more fully through worship, serving, growing in knowledge of Him, and fellowship with other believers.

Up until this point in your life, you may have lived in a home where church attendance was just as much a routine for you as brushing your teeth. But come post-graduation, this will change. If you are moving to another city after graduation, will be serving in the military, or are headed off to college, the emphasis (and effort) you place upon church attendance will take on a whole new meaning, if for no other reason than because Mom won't be there anymore to get her little darling out of bed for Sunday school.

You don't have to make the choice of *where* you go to church after graduating today. But you need to solidify in your mind the choice of *whether* you go to church after graduation now! Being confident in your beliefs about church will help you make the right choice about where and how often you will attend.

1. What kind of church should I attend?

Answering this question requires asking more questions. Finding the church God has called you to may take some time and will take patience. But asking the right questions along the way is important:

What church does God want me to attend?
I can't answer this question for you. Even you can't answer this question for you. Only God can. So focus on prayer as you consider what church to attend. If you give this over to God and ask for His wisdom, He will show you.

What denomination of church should I attend?
There are many different beliefs among churches, and denomination isn't as important as beliefs. Still, a denominational affiliation may be important to you. Regardless, I encourage you to Google various church denominations of interest to you and research each.

One of the first things you should do when you visit a church is to find out what the church believes. Talk to a pastor about the church's doctrinal beliefs. Meet with elders. Check out the church's website, blogs, and podcasts. Every church should have a mission statement or a statement of faith, and church leaders should be able to clearly articulate their beliefs to you. The bottom line is, they must be a Christian church that believes and unequivocally teaches salvation through Jesus Christ alone.

How is God calling me to serve in the church?
Worship style, attire, décor, and more are all issues you may want to consider when choosing a church. But more important

than the style of worship, suit or jeans, and organ or guitar is your consideration of service.

Psalm 22:22 (NIV) says, "I will declare your name to my brothers; in the congregation I will praise you." So be careful not to fall into the trap of attending church for what church will do for you. One of the greatest privileges of going to church is to serve God—to bring Him glory, just like my drummer friend in Nashville is doing!

Look at Psalm 134:1-2 (MSG): "Come, bless GOD, all you servants of GOD.... In GOD's shrine, lift your praising hands to the Holy Place." As you plug in to a church to bring God glory, He will plug you in to places of service where you will impact the lives of others and honor Him.

What questions should I ask before joining a church?
Make a list of things that are important to you in a church and find the answers to such questions as these: Does this church preach the Word of God? Does this church encourage fellowship and community? Does this church support the outreach of missionaries nationally and globally? Does this church encourage financial accountability and giving?

2. How often should I attend church?

How often you attend isn't as important as being genuinely involved in the church.

After high school, your church-attending schedule may fluctuate from week to week and month to month as you adjust to your new life on the other side of the cap and gown. But make church a priority in your life. If you don't do this from the beginning, life will become more and more busy and church will become less and less a part of your life.

3. Is it important for me to support my church financially?

No, it isn't important. It is essential!

Many struggle with the issue of tithing. In "The Money Game" chapter, Robby tackles this issue in greater detail as it relates to establishing a budget. I mention it here because it is important to take this into consideration when joining and serving your church. Check out God's words in Malachi 3:8 (NIV) to people who weren't tithing:

> Will a man rob God? Yet you rob me.
> But you ask, "How do we rob you?"
> In tithes and offerings.

The New Testament also talks about the importance of giving and about the fact that we are expected to seek God's will in this matter as we give a portion of our income back to the church. In 2 Corinthians 9:6-7 (MSG) we read, "Remember: A stingy planter gets a stingy crop; a lavish planter gets a lavish crop. I want each of you to take plenty of time to think it over, and make up your own mind what you will give. That will protect you against sob stories and arm-twisting. God loves it when the giver delights in the giving."

Supporting your church financially is just one of your acts of worship. I promise that if you do it, God will bless you more than you can ever imagine!

HOLDING STRONG

"What is truth?" Pilate asked in John 18:38 (NIV).

Jesus was on trial for His life. Pilate was the one man who had the authority to condemn Jesus to death or set Him free. The chief priests were demanding that Jesus be crucified. John 19:8 says that Pilate "was even more afraid" when he heard the demands of the Jewish leaders to have Jesus killed. By this point in the story, Scripture shows us how, on three different occasions, Pilate had stated to these Jewish leaders that he could find no basis for a charge against Jesus. But John 19:16 reads, "Finally Pilate handed [Jesus] over to them to be crucified." He said he believed Jesus was innocent. His actions, however, proved that his confidence was in his popularity and position as Roman governor rather than in what he said he believed about Jesus. Pilate was more tempted to appease the crowd than honor God.

Although it is impossible at this point for you to know what you believe about everything, it is critical for you to know what you believe about God. Is God just religion for you, or have you surrendered your life to Him by believing in His Son, Jesus, and accepting Him as Lord? Your beliefs about God, religion, and Christianity will shape *all* of your beliefs. And, as it was with Pilate, if you are not confident in what you believe, it will only be a matter of time before the crowd sways your beliefs.

Know what you believe about religion. Know what you believe about church. Know what you believe about God. If you are basing these beliefs in the infallible Word of God, you will be laying a foundation for your life that will never be moved.

Dear God,
I pray that I will grow in confidence in Your Word and who You are. I pray that, as I commit more time to Your Word, it will become alive in me. I pray that You will lead me to the right church where I can be used by You and serve You and others. Protect me from the lies of Satan, who would have me believe that there are many ways to You. Give me confidence to trust You more and to help lead those under my influence to do the same. Amen.

Chapter 3

What Do I Believe About Relationships?

Jeffrey Dean

Consider these questions:

- Are family relationships important to me? Why or why not?
- Do I work hard to maintain healthy relationships with my family and my friends?
- Do I value time with my sibling(s)?
- What are some of the greatest challenges I face in my dating relationships?
- Do I believe my relationships have an impact on my choices, my lifestyle, and my convictions?

You probably know by now that figuring out relationships isn't easy. Relationships—*all* of them—take work! But with that work comes the reward of living in and experiencing community with others.

This chapter is broken into three main categories of relationships: family, friends, and dating. In the next five years of your life, you will be challenged in many different ways in all three of these categories. As you are, my hope is that you will gain a greater understanding of the importance of maintaining and growing your relationships with your family, friends, and those interesting people of the opposite sex who catch your eye. Start planning to have healthy relationships now, and God will release His direction for how to live life with others in ways that honor Him and fit with the unique kind of individual He created you to be.

WHAT DO I BELIEVE ABOUT FAMILY RELATIONSHIPS?

But whether you have strong relationships with your family members or not, the truth is that your family is your family. As you begin to stretch your graduate wings and fly, remember that God gave you the family you have. Just because graduation comes and goes doesn't mean you have the freedom to go...and rarely come back.

Murder, lying, lust, betrayal, incest, and rape. Sounds like a Hollywood blockbuster, doesn't it? Actually, these are words that could describe the Bible's stories of family funk.

For instance, there's the one about the Bible's first siblings, Cain and Abel. In anger, Cain lures his brother into the fields and then murders him (Genesis 4:1-16).

Then there's the story about the twins Esau and Jacob. Esau trades a bowl of stew to his brother in exchange for a birthright from their father. He later realizes his foolishness and holds a grudge against his brother, saying, "The days of mourning for my father are near; then I will kill my brother Jacob" (Genesis 27:41, NIV).

Joseph's brothers consider killing him but instead sell him into slavery. They then lie about it, kill a goat, dip Joseph's robe in it, and tell their father, "We found this. Examine it to see whether it is your son's robe" (Genesis 37:32, NIV).

And don't forget the story about a brother in 2 Samuel 13 who rapes his sister. A family feud breaks out and leads to betrayal, death, and more.

Talk about drama. And all of this happened within the first nine books of the Bible!

Hopefully your family isn't dealing with this kind of stuff. But if your family is like most families, then you probably do have some kind of drama that's a big deal to you. You don't need me to tell you that family life is challenging.

But whether you have strong relationships with your family members or not, the truth is that your family is your family. As you begin to stretch your graduate wings and fly, remember that God gave you the family you have. Just because graduation comes and goes doesn't mean you have the freedom to go…and rarely come back.

A friend of mine graduated from high school and told me he was "outta here!" He left for college soon after and rarely called home or went home. It wasn't until fall break of his freshman year (two months after leaving for college) that he came home. Well, actually, when he came home, he didn't go home. He stayed at a friend's house nearby. It wasn't until Sunday morning of fall break, when he attended church, that he actually saw and spoke to his parents. Needless to say, his parents were crushed.

I'm a big believer that you need a little space after graduating to just be you. But excluding your parents from that process is a foolish—and selfish—move on your part.

Family is very important to God. Why do you think He calls Himself *the Father* and Jesus *the Son*? Why does He call us His *children*? Because He knows the bond between family members is one of the greatest and strongest this world can offer. Throughout the Bible, we see time and again the value God places on family.

Proverbs 31 talks about a wife and mother providing for her family. First Timothy 3 highlights the importance of providing for family. Then 1 Timothy 5:8 (NIV) says, "If anyone does not provide for his relatives, and especially for his immediate family, he has denied the faith and is worse than an unbeliever."

It's evident that God expects us to be pro-family, especially when it comes to our parents!

Relationships with Your Parents

I realize that you may not have grown up under the influence of both of your parents. When I'm on the road speaking, I meet young adults every day whose parents are divorced, deceased, or never got married in the first place. I remember a few years ago meeting Rick, an eighteen year old whose dad left his mom when Rick was three. I met Rick when he was still living with his mother, who was not very involved in his life. "She jumps from relationship to relationship with a lot of men," Rick said, "and seldom makes the time to even acknowledge my existence."

Rick stands out to me from the many young adults I meet like Rick because of his determination to not repeat the parenting practices of his mom and dad. He said, "They haven't been the best parents to me. I guess you could say they both failed me. I sure want to learn from their mistakes and be the best dad I can be to my children one day."

Regardless of how you would define your parents' parenting skills, God's Word is clear on His expectations of you and your role as a child. Exodus 20:12 (NIV) says, "Honor your father and your mother." There's no mistaking what God is saying in that verse. Does it say to honor them unless they've bailed on you? Does it say to honor them unless you disagree with them? Does it say to honor them unless you think they no longer deserve it? Does it say to honor them until you graduate? No! It just says to honor them. Period.

So, how do you honor Mom and Dad post-graduation? Well, the list is endless. But one way you can do so is summed up in the word *recognition*. Since the moment good ol' Mom and Dad saw you for the first time, they've probably been spending a whole lot of time focused more on you than on themselves. They watched you go through a lot of milestones and seasons of life:

- pacifiers, baby bottles, pooping in your pants (hopefully you are over this one)
- your first words, your first bike ride, and your first day of every year of school
- ball practice, dance lessons, and an insane number of trips to the store for new clothes
- *Barney*, *The Wiggles*, and *Hannah Montana* (you know you listened)

- date nights, late nights, and prom night
- bone breaks, spring breaks, and heartbreaks!

Your parents have given a lot to help you become who you are today. Recognize this and keep remembering it your entire life!

Practical Ways to Honor Your Parents

1. Be there.
Just because you may not be living at home anymore doesn't mean you can't come back home. If possible, get back to see your family regularly. Even if you can't get home from school, work, or other obligations often, sharing a little love is only a phone call, Skype, or FaceTime away.

2. Write a note.
In my office I have a box of letters my girls have written to me. One I received when my oldest daughter turned seven. It reads, "Dear Daddy, I love you very much. I will always be your best friend forever. And one day I want to marry you!" (Cute now—freaky when she's nineteen!) I cherish the letters my girls give to me. I hope they never stop writing them.

Maybe you haven't been the letter-writing type. But you can be now. It's amazing what writing a quick note or e-mail to someone does, especially from a child to a parent.

3. Pray.
Maybe your mom, dad, or both haven't been the parent(s) that you wanted them to be or that they should have been. Maybe one or both aren't Christ followers. Well, the command to *honor* them in Scripture isn't contingent upon their parenting abilities or salvation.

"How do I honor a parent who hasn't given his or her life to the Lord?" you may be asking.

The answer: prayer.

There is no greater act of honor one can give to another than praying for that person. Whether you define your parents as having been perfect or less than perfect, honor them by praying for them.

And look what God says when you choose to be a child who honors Mom and Dad: "Obey your father and your mother, and you will have a long and happy life" (Ephesians 6:2, CEV).

Relationships with Your Brothers and Sisters

Okay, so what about siblings? Do you have one or two or more? If so, you could probably write a book about the sibling challenges you have experienced. I know I can.

Make the most of the time while you are still sharing a home with your sibling. Even if your relationship with your sibling is rocky, mark my words: there will come a time later in life when you miss what you now have with your sibling.

I have two brothers—one older, one younger. We love one another like crazy. There were also times growing up when we would fight like crazy. I wish someone had told me then what I'm about to tell you now. So listen up, grad!

My brother Kent is one year older than me. I idolized him in high school. (Still kind of do today!) Kent was the coolest guy on campus. Everyone knew him and looked up to him. He lettered in every sport our school offered from his freshman through senior year. He was senior class VP and voted "Mr. RHS" upon graduation. I still remember the day my parents dropped him off at college. It was only an hour away from our home, but to me it was like he was moving halfway around the world. I cried. A lot.

The reality that things would never be the same again hit me pretty hard in those first few weeks after he left. You may not view your sibling(s) exactly the same as I do mine. But sooner rather than later, you will no longer share a home with your sibling. Sooner rather than later, you will not have the privilege of seeing your sibling every day. Sooner rather than later, you and your sibling will most likely have your own homes, with your own spouse and children, living your own lives. Even if you are fortunate enough to live your adult life in the same city as a sibling, your relationship will never again be as it is right now. Make the most of the time while you are still sharing a home with your sibling. Even if your relationship with your sibling is rocky, mark my words: there will come a time later in life when you miss what you now have with your sibling.

WHAT DO I BELIEVE ABOUT FRIEND RELATIONSHIPS?

Friendships. We all have them. We all want them. And, to a certain extent, we all need them. Your world of friendships is one of the, if not the most, powerful influences in your life today. But do you ever really think about the friendships you have and how they affect you? Have you put a lot of consideration into choosing good, Christian friends, or do you simply search for acceptance from the most popular, the coolest, or the most exciting?

The friends you choose throughout the next few years of your life won't simply be people you know. They will most likely be the friends you choose for life. They'll be people you do life with. Choose wisely!

The friends you choose throughout the next few years of your life won't simply be people you know. They will most likely be the friends you choose for life. They'll be people you do *life* with. Choose wisely!

The more time you spend with another person, the more that person influences you. That's natural. You probably like bands your friends introduced you to in high school. And you've probably played your favorite video game a million or two times with some of your closest friends. As you commit time to a friend, that person's influence affects your lifestyle more and more. Think about it: On your "Top 10 Greatest Moments of My High School Career" list, you probably did some pretty fun and crazy things. (My list includes a cold Saturday night over Christmas break that includes a pick-up truck full of friends, about four dozen rolls of toilet paper, and a late-night trip to our basketball coach's front yard. Needless to say, it was a surprise visit!)

If your list is like mine, then it probably includes a lot of time making memories with your closest friends that you wish you could just erase. On your "Top 10 Most Regrettable Moments of My High School Career" list, some of your biggest moments of regret probably involved a friend or friends: prom night, spring break, at a party, on a date. As 1 Corinthians 15:33 (NIV) says, "Do not be misled: 'Bad company corrupts character.'"

What's the point?

To put it simply, influence equals character. Who you spend time with shapes the choices you make and ultimately the person you become.

Many years ago I found a great verse, Proverbs 13:20, which says everything God wants us to know about choosing healthy friendships. I hope you'll read it and remember it when you begin to make new relationships post–high school: "He who walks with the wise grows wise, but a companion of fools suffers harm" (NIV).

There are two things I want you to make sure you see in this passage. The first is a promise. I love it when I read God's promises in the Bible, because I know that when He offers us a promise, He keeps it! Look at the promise: "He who walks with the wise grows wise." So the obvious question is, what does it mean to be *wise*? The obvious answer is that a wise person is someone who knows the difference between right and wrong and chooses to do what's right. If you choose to live by this proverb, spending time with people who know right from wrong and choose right, you're going to grow wise.

Second is the warning, and it is just as clear as the promise: "A companion of fools suffers harm." If you hang out with fools, then bad stuff is going to happen to you. This verse doesn't say bad stuff "might happen" or that it "very well could happen." God's Word is completely clear. It says you *will* suffer harm. So, if you make the choice to hang out with fools, it's not a question of *if* you'll get hurt but *when*.

Of course, not only do you need to *pursue* the wise, but also you need to *be* the wise to others. Be the wise by being you. In the days ahead, there will be moments when your reputation, grades, income, status, and more may be on the line. Choosing to lose yourself in the moment, or gain something in the moment, may seem right in the moment. But becoming someone other than who God desires you to be will never be right and will never honor Him.

Several weeks into my first freshman semester of college, I went to hear a band with several new friends I had made. All of us were new to Nashville and we wanted to go hear a local band that we were told was really good. We *thought* we were only going to see a band on stage that night. But before the band took the stage to play, several topless women walked out on stage and started dancing! My seventeen-year-old eyes had never seen anything like this before. We were all shocked. For a period of time that seemed like forever (but that I'm sure was just a few moments) none of us had moved. I finally stood up and said, "Let's go." Everyone followed me out and we laughed about that for a long time. I'm so glad I didn't choose to stay.

As you meet and choose new friends, stay true to who you are. Also, remember that life isn't about having loads of people you barely know *friend* you on Facebook. Proverbs 18:24 (NIV) says, "A man of many companions may come to ruin, but there is a friend who sticks closer than a brother." Rather than competing to be everybody's friend, be wise in choosing a few close friends who you can do life with. Meaningful friendships don't always come easily. And there will be times when distinguishing between healthy and unhealthy friendships will be hard. But as you commit to stay in consistent communication with God, He'll give you wisdom to know the difference.

Here are several questions for your consideration:

1. Should I be friends with a non-Christian?

This is a tricky one. Check out what 2 Corinthians 6:14-16 (MSG) says:

> Don't become partners with those who reject God. How can you make a partnership out of right and wrong? That's not partnership; that's war. Is light best friends with dark? Does Christ go strolling with the Devil? Do trust and mistrust hold hands? Who would think of setting up pagan idols in God's holy Temple? But that is exactly what we are, each of us a temple in whom God lives.

It's one thing to know a non-Christian. I know many. I spend time with these people in my neighborhood, at family events, and more. But I am careful not to call these people "friends." My hope is that my life-influence will point these people to Christ. But I am also reminded of the warning of 2 Corinthians 6.

I know this can be a difficult principle to live by. But look at the rest of this passage.

God himself put it this way:

> "I'll live in them, move into them; I'll be their God and they'll be my people. So leave the corruption and compromise; leave it for good," says God. "Don't link up with those who will pollute you. I want you all for myself. I'll be a Father to you; you'll be sons and daughters to me."

When I read this whole passage, I see that God is labeling my friendship with a nonbeliever as a partnership with *wrong, darkness, corrup-*

tion, and *compromise!* These are not the kinds of words that come to mind for me when I think about my friendships.

2. Is it okay to room with someone of the opposite sex?

First Thessalonians 5:22 (NIV) says, "Avoid every kind of evil." Even if you aren't sleeping together, the appearance of it can damage your Christian witness. Not only that, but no matter how pure your intentions going into the arrangement might be, sharing a home with someone of the opposite sex can be tempting. Why place yourself in a position such as this one that can lead to compromise?

WHAT DO I BELIEVE ABOUT DATING RELATIONSHIPS?

There is so much I could write about concerning dating, purity, and marriage. This book is not intended to tackle these issues in great detail. There is, however, a strong possibility that you will date and meet your life mate (if you haven't already done so) in the next five years of your life. If you have not been confronted with the choice of sex as of yet, consider yourself fortunate. If you think you are immune to this confrontation in the immediate future, think again.

I recently read an interesting article about the effects of sugar in the body. You know the sensation you experience when you lick your favorite flavor of ice cream or bite into that hot, steamy Krispy Kreme donut. (If you don't know Krispy Kreme donuts, your tongue doesn't know amazing!) Well, some might believe that the pleasure of such sweet delights is only experienced by the sensation of sucrose hitting the tongue. But not so. The fact is, you continue to taste sugar as it works its way through your body.

Taste cells specialized to detect sweet-tasting stuff live all over the tongue. When something sweet hits these cells, a *Yum!* signal is sent right to the brain. As you digest sugar, enzymes break it all down into glucose and fructose. In the small intestine, some of these same taste cells that are on the tongue are present there too. The result, once again, is *Yum!* Out of the small intestine, transporter proteins carry these molecules through the bloodstream to the pancreas. And guess what? Yes, in the pancreas, the same reaction: *Yum! Yum!*

The point is, the sugar sensation we have all experienced is a full-body one.

And, you guessed it, the same is true when it comes to sex.

Sex is a full-person—physical, emotional, and spiritual—experience! That's how God made it. And just like the "Oh my word!" moment you have when your body gets a hit of your favo sugar-fix, God wants you to experience the same when it comes to the gift of sex. He created you as a sexual being to enjoy sex the way He intended it to be: one man + one woman within a marriage for life!

Again, this is not a sex and love chapter, but I can't talk straight with you about the next five years of your life without giving you a few things to think about when it comes to dating. After almost two decades of counseling with thousands, I have met many God-loving, in-Jesus-believing, church-attending young adults who have made poor choices in this area of their lives during the first few years after graduation from high school.

1. Is it okay to date a non-Christian?

Let me answer this question with a few more questions for you to consider:

- Would you want to marry someone who doesn't believe there's a heaven, hell, or God?
- Would you want to marry someone who wouldn't embrace reading the Bible, going to church, and praying?
- Would you want to marry someone who wouldn't instill in your children godly character and the practices of praying, going to church, and reading the Bible?

I hope the answer to each of these questions would be a definite no from you. If this is the case, then why would you choose to date someone who wouldn't do these things?

Anyone you choose to date should be marriage worthy. Don't fall into the trap of believing *If I date this person, I can change this person.* I know of countless stories that have tragically proven otherwise.

2. Is it okay to have sex with my boyfriend or girlfriend?

You need to know that Satan knows about the sugar thing. He knows that once you get a taste of it, you'll want more! And he will work like mad to dangle the goods in front of you and get you to believe the lie that the choice to have sex before marriage is no big deal.

Satan wants you to be confused about God's plan for your sex life. He wants you to believe that the Bible hasn't clearly outlined what's okay and what's not when it comes to sex. He wants you to think there are all kinds of loopholes in God's rules that allow you to do some things that aren't technically sex. But he's wrong. Dead wrong. God's Word is clear: impurity is off limits.

There are tons of reasons to not cross the purity line until you're married—reasons like guilt, unwanted pregnancy, STDs, and bed partner comparisons. But the ultimate reason you need to believe that sex until marriage is no good is because God said so!

So, what if this hasn't been your protocol thus far?

It's never too late for you to do the right thing. If you've made wrong sexual choices, you can start over. You can come clean with yourself, come clean with God, and make the choice now that God's way will be your will from now on. "If we confess our sins to God, he can always be trusted to forgive us and take our sins away" (1 John 1:9, CEV).

When it comes to your dating life, make it your goal now to stick to God's way of purity. First Corinthians 6:18 (NIV) says, "Flee from sexual immorality." You don't need me to explain that there will be many moments of challenge waiting for you on your college campus, in the workplace, and more. Being determined to do right doesn't exempt you from temptation. But it does place you one step ahead of the challenge. So be determined to...

- Never compromise who you are or who you choose to date.
- Clearly articulate your expectations and intentions for any dating relationship before your first date.
- Decide now what type of parties you won't go to, movies you won't watch, and environments you won't step into.
- Say no!
- Walk away from any relationship that hinders your relationship with God.

3. What does the Bible say about same-sex attraction?

Culture screams an entirely different message than Scripture on many issues, but especially this one. Several of the biggest shows on prime-time TV now promote homosexuality, lesbianism, bisexuality, and experimentation with it all. Same-sex behavior is more accepted in our society now, and saying that it's wrong can make you seem intolerant. And if people think you're intolerant, they're less likely to listen to what you have to say. But you also can't ignore what God's Word says.

Maybe you, or someone you know, have been in a same-sex relationship. If so, then you probably believe or have friends who believe that homosexuals are born with same-sex attraction and that they didn't choose to be gay. I don't see anywhere in Scripture where God says that He created anyone to be homosexual. It's a sin and it's not part of God's plan. However, knowing this, believing this, or saying this to someone is not as easy as me writing it in this book. I get that. But I also get that we can't ignore God's Word just because it doesn't justify a lifestyle choice such as this. Scripture states clearly that it's wrong:

> God let them follow their own evil desires. Women no longer wanted to have sex in a natural way, and they did things

with each other that were not natural. Men behaved in the same way. They stopped wanting to have sex with women and had strong desires for sex with other men. They did shameful things with each other, and what has happened to them is punishment for their foolish deeds. (Romans 1:26-27, CEV)

If you are living the homosexual lifestyle, I hope that you will continue reading this book, even if you don't agree with what I've written about this topic. I also hope that you won't close the door to allowing God to speak to you about this choice you are making. Believe this: God loves you like crazy. And I believe He has a better plan for you than the one you are living in now. I hope you will keep taking this to Him and let His Word show you that there is a way out of this lifestyle.

If you know someone who is struggling with this lifestyle, the best thing to do is remember that you're not anyone's judge. Only God can judge others properly. So when you are confronted (notice I didn't say *if* you are confronted) by a professor, a friend, a co-worker, or a roommate, this will help you be more humble when you share parts of God's Word that aren't so welcome to some people. All you can do when you're faced with issues like homosexuality is to let people know what the Bible says—and also to let them know that you love them. It may seem impossible to do both at the same time, but God's got a knack for making the impossible possible. All you have to do is ask for His help.

If you know someone who is struggling with homosexuality and isn't sure what to do about those feelings, you need to let this person know that he or she is not alone. Be someone this person can talk to. Then talk to this person about the importance of relying on God's Word. Explain that God loves him or her completely. Such a struggle is no surprise to God, and He desires to help anyone break free of it. Encourage this person to talk to Him and ask for strength and guidance. And stress the importance of finding a Christian counselor who can also help. You may even choose to help this person find someone who will be both honest and kind.

A LIFELONG EXERCISE

It is God's desire that you learn to trust Him more and more with your relationships. This will be a lifelong exercise as you learn to rely on God to lead you in your relationships with family, friends, and dating. (And yes, dating continues even after you are married. But, no, not with multiple dating relationships. I'm talking about dating your spouse here. A heads-up to all the guys out there—don't forget this one!) In the next five years of your life, you will be challenged in many different ways in all three of these categories. Don't stop taking this to God. Don't allow spiritual apathy to set in here. You can't do it God's way if you don't give God access to these relationships. Keep praying that God will lead you with *His* wisdom in your relationships and that He will release His direction in this area of your life so that you will learn to honor Him.

> *Dear God,*
> *I pray that I will learn to rely on You to lead me as I choose my relationships. Help me to surround myself with people who push me closer to You rather than pull me away from You. I pray that whatever is true, whatever is noble, whatever is right, whatever is pure, whatever is lovely, whatever is admirable—if anything is excellent or praiseworthy—I would think about such things. I pray that You will protect me from an impure life. I pray that I will honor You in all of my relationships, particularly in my dating life. I pray that You will bring me friends that desire to honor You with sex, love, and dating. Give me the courage to stand for what is right in my relationships, even when others don't. Teach me to be the kind of person that points others to You, and I pray that my friends, family, and dates see You in me. Amen.*

Chapter 4

The Money Game

Robby McGee

Brittany, a twenty year old, wrote me to say, "I am amazed at how many things really have changed since graduating from high school." She admitted that she had never put much thought into her finances while in high school. Now, just two years after graduation, she was about to make some decisions that would affect her life for many years.

She said, "I now realize how much my parents did for me. My dad bought my first car. But now I need a new one. I'm about to buy a car and lock in to a monthly payment for the next five years. This will be a little tricky because I will not be driving this car at all next summer. I am studying abroad and obviously won't be taking my car with me. Also, I have to start saving now for the additional expenses I will have while being out of the country. I want to be smart with my decisions. I don't want to make the wrong move and start something that will hurt me down the road for years to come."

Brittany was right. The decisions you will be faced with post-graduation will be unlike many, if any, you've been forced to make before. And these decisions will have a huge impact on your life from this point forward. Whether that impact turns out to be positive or negative will be greatly influenced by many of the financial decisions you make over the next three to five years. During this time, it is very possible that you will:

- Borrow money to go to college.
- Purchase or finance a new laptop for college or work.
- Buy a new car.
- Apply for one or more credit cards.
- Buy a house.
- Save for retirement.

What does it really mean to be a steward? I define it this way: managing God's stuff in God's way for God's purposes.

There is no doubt that these and other financial decisions can become overwhelming. This is why Jeffrey and I keep pointing your attention back to the Word. As you've read throughout this book, the Word is the key to your success moving forward. This is critically important as it pertains to your financial decisions. And this is why I love Psalm 24:1. It is a foundational truth about money and possessions that can change your life forever! Check it out: "The earth is the LORD's, and everything in it, the world, and all who live in it" (NIV). Simply put, it's all God's stuff. We're just stewards!

I know what you may be thinking. *I've heard that before.* Exactly! But whether you've heard it before or not, the key is not hearing it. It's believing it—and living like you believe it!

So, what does it really mean to be a steward? I define it this way: managing God's stuff in God's way for God's purposes.

Imagine God showing up on your next payday, paying you in cash, and saying, "I'm counting on you to manage this wisely and spend it according to My principles. Whatever you spend the money on, make sure you put My purposes ahead of your own." Okay, so if God really showed up at your front door with a handful of cash, how would you respond? After picking your jaw up off the ground (actually, you'd probably be picking up more than just your jaw), you'd probably spend your money a little differently that week. I know I would!

When my son went away to start his first semester of college, I thought my wife and I had prepared him to be out on his own, to manage money wisely, and to live within a budget. After all, not only had we modeled it for him, but we had also encouraged him to be wise in saving and practical in spending. For example, when he was twelve, we helped him create a budget and started giving him cash twice a month to manage according to his budget.

So you can imagine my surprise when he called me from college and said, "Hey, Dad, you know how sometimes, even though you have been taught and believe something is wrong, you have to end up proving it to yourself anyway?" He went on to tell me that when he opened up his checking account, the bank gave him a credit card to go along with it. Instead of putting it away and continuing to pay for everything with cash or a check (which is what we had always encouraged him to do), he started using it. Before he knew it, he had racked up over $800 on the card, mostly on food and clothes. Although he had a meal ticket to eat on campus and plenty of clothes, he had fallen victim to some of the common money mistakes many make shortly after leaving home and getting out on their own. What my son, like Brittany, quickly realized was that money decisions matter and can be costly if made poorly.

This chapter provides you with some basic, practical steps about managing God's stuff in God's way for God's purposes. This includes having a budget, avoiding debt, and saving for the future. It is my hope that, by reading about them, you can avoid the consequences of making many of the common money mistakes. Remember, planning releases God's direction. So planning how you will implement time-tested money management principles will help to provide the resources you need to accomplish God's financial plan for your life.

A budget is not about the amount of money you have; it's about what you do with the money you have, regardless of the amount.

THE BUDGET

God expects you to wisely manage the money He provides. And in order to manage wisely, you need a plan. A budget is simply a written plan that determines how you are going to use God's resources. It tracks the money coming in and the money going out.

Can you imagine a company operating without a written budget? How long do you think the company would be in business with unrestrained spending in every department, regardless of the company's income? Your household is like a small business. And your household, just like a company, will be unsuccessful without a written spending plan based upon income.

Now, I know what you might be saying (if I've heard it once, I've heard it a thousand times): "I don't have enough money to budget."

However, a budget is not about the amount of money you have; it's about what you do with the money you have, regardless of the amount. A budget is there to help you prioritize your spending, control impulse buying and emotional spending, establish your short- and long-term goals, and provide for those little emergencies that will inevitably pop up throughout your life.

Do I need a budget?

I believe everybody needs a budget, no matter how much or how little they may make. It helps you to keep from living beyond your means if money is tight, and it helps you to wisely manage God's resources when it's not.

Several years ago I taught a class on budgeting at my church. One man in the class informed me that he didn't see the need for a written budget. He said that he had more than enough income to cover his expenses and he always had plenty of money left at the end of every month. Within twelve months, the economy had taken a dive and I heard that he had filed for bankruptcy.

Unfortunately, I have seen this type of story played out time and time again with people who, for various reasons, didn't see the need for a budget. In almost every instance, a budget (which includes saving for emergencies) would have helped these people avoid their financial crisis.

How can a budget help me?

One of the main things a budget will help you do is spend money on purpose. Although most people think they know where their money goes, without a budget—they don't! Just think about it: If I asked you to account for everything you had spent money on in the last thirty days, would you really know? More importantly, would you be able to give an accounting to God?

Robert, a youth pastor, came to me and asked if I would meet with him about his financial situation. He had gotten into quite a bit of debt and was having a hard time making ends meet. I discovered during our meeting that he didn't really have an income problem; he had a spending problem. I helped him put together a budget, and when he left our meeting, he was excited about getting his finances in order.

A year later we met again. Robert confessed that he had not implemented his budget, and his financial position had worsened. I asked him to track every penny he spent for the next thirty days and then meet with me again.

Thirty days later, he and I were surprised at the results. We discovered he had been spending almost $300 per month hitting soda machines and getting a sugar rush on soft drinks and candy bars alone. I asked him if he felt like he was managing God's stuff in God's way for God's purposes. The answer was obvious!

This time he got serious about implementing a budget and properly managing God's stuff. Less than two years later, he was almost completely out of debt and had money in the bank for emergencies. Was this an easy fix for Robert? No! He had to take a hard look at reality and then be committed to a lifestyle adjustment. But the result was worth the sacrifice.

How do I get started?

We have included a budget worksheet online at www.thegraduatehandbook.com as a road map to help you create your budget. The good news is, all the skills you need to create a budget you learned in elementary school—reading, writing, and arithmetic!

The first thing to do is make a list of *all* your monthly expenses. One way to help compile totals for your monthly expenses is to review your checkbook, debit card statements, and any credit card statements for the last ninety days. Remember, some bills are due quarterly (such as car insurance) or even annually (such as car tags). You would be surprised at some of the items that are often overlooked and not accounted for when creating a budget. The goal here is to find out what you spend annually and to break it down into smaller monthly amounts.

After accounting for all of your expenses, enter them into the budget worksheet, add them all up, and subtract the total from your monthly income. If you see that you are spending more than you make, you will have to make adjustments to your expenses (or income) in order to balance. If you see that you are spending less than you make, assign that money to start an emergency fund, contribute to a retirement fund, or pursue some other long-term savings goal.

The objective of the worksheet is to assign all of the money coming in to a line item on the worksheet. When the ending balance on the worksheet is zero, you have taken the first step in spending with purpose!

How do I implement my budget?

The simplest part of the budgeting process is writing it down. The challenge can be putting it into practice. Know this: it takes around ninety days to successfully implement a budget. So don't get frustrated with your short-term progress. Keep your eye on the prize by reminding yourself that this is the best way for you to manage God's stuff in God's way for God's purposes.

Although the points below use physical budget sheets and envelopes, there are also several budget and virtual envelope apps available. The budget apps help you to keep track of your budget electronically, and the virtual envelope apps provide you with a virtual envelope for each expense to help you track your cash or debit card spending. When the virtual envelope hits zero, you're done for that period! Just search online or at your favorite app store and try one out!

Now let's get to the three main keys to putting a budget into practice.

1. Assign a portion of every paycheck you receive to a line item on the budget.

To do this, simply take every item on your budget and divide it by the number of paychecks you are going to receive for the current month. This will give you the portion of each check that you need to set aside for each line item. For instance, if your rent is $500 per month and you get paid twice a month, then you would set aside $250 from each check to cover the rent. If your cell phone bill is $100 per month, you would set aside $50 from each check. And so on.

2. Use the cash envelope system for every expense that is not a fixed expense.

The cash envelope system can be very effective in helping you implement your budget. Here's how it works.

Beside each line item on your budget worksheet downloaded from our website, you will see an F or a C. Those items with an F are your fixed expenses, and those items with a C are your cash expenses. The fixed expenses tend to be more constant, and your cash expenses will tend to fluctuate. The goal is to pay all of the F expenses by debit card or check and all of the C expenses with cash. Step one in using the cash envelope system is to take one envelope for each line item on your budget worksheet that has a C beside it and write the name of that line item on the envelope. Step two is to take the proper amount of cash as determined from your budget worksheet and place it in each envelope. Step three is to make the amount of cash in the envelope last until you receive your next paycheck.

Here's an example. Let's say you get paid twice a month and the line item on your budget for food is $200 per month, gas is $150 per month, entertainment is $50 per month, and miscellaneous is $50 per month. When you get paid, you would take $225 cash out of the bank (the total of those monthly budget amounts divided by two since you get paid twice a month) and put $100 in your food envelope, $75 in your gas envelope, $25 in your entertainment envelope, and $25 in your miscellaneous envelope. When the money in each envelope is gone, this means the pair of jeans you are dying to get into will have to wait until next month, because you're done until the next paycheck!

Keep in mind that, in the initial months, you may have to make adjustments to the amounts you have allocated for each line item on your budget worksheet in order to make it work.

3. Discipline yourself not to spend money that is not in the budget. The entitlement mentality in our culture can make following this key principle the greatest road block to implementing your budget, especially if your income is barely enough to cover your basic needs. Remember, budgeting is just simple math. If you spend more than you make, you have to end up borrowing; and if you end up borrowing (a topic that we will cover later), it always (that's right, *always*) ends up creating a problem at some point. The principle is simple: If it isn't in your budget, don't spend money on it. If you use the cash envelope system and only use a debit card or write checks for the other line items in your budget, it has to work, barring some financial crisis that could not be planned for. (Although there are some exceptions, almost every financial crisis is only a crisis due to poor planning and/or poor decisions.)

You can be sure that at some point you are going to be pressured to spend money that is not in your budget. Whether it is a friend wanting you to go to a movie, a co-worker asking you to go out for lunch, or your family wanting you to come home and visit when you don't have the money for the gas or airfare, trust me, there will be plenty of well-meaning people pulling at you to spend money you don't have!

A twenty-something woman once told me that she could not stay on her budget because her co-workers were always asking her to chip in on a wedding shower, baby shower, or birthday party. Her budget was fairly tight, and although she didn't really have the money to do it, she was afraid of what the others would think of her if she didn't participate.

I told her, "The next time they ask you to chip in, tell them that, although you would love to help out, you have already made financial obligations to other people and that it would not be right for you to chip in and not be able to fulfill those obligations."

The next time I saw her, she couldn't wait to tell me what had happened. Not only did her co-workers not think badly of her; they were actually relieved. Her response had given them the freedom to say no too! It turns out, many of them were only participating out of guilt and didn't have the money either.

DEBT

Credit cards, car loans, college loans, computer loans, furniture loans, keeping-up-with-the-newest-nail-art-trends loans (okay, that one is pushing it)…stop the insanity! To date, the total amount of outstanding college debt has surpassed $1 trillion, the total credit card debt is just over $800 billion dollars, and depending on what statistic you choose, from 85 to 90 percent of car sales are financed.

I don't think anyone will argue that debt is commonplace in our culture. But regardless, debt is, has been, and always will be a trap. Proverbs 22:7 (NIV) puts it this way: "The rich rule over the poor, and the borrower is servant to the lender." So, if someone came up to you and said, "I will give you a loan for one thousand dollars, but you have to agree to be enslaved to me until you pay it back," would you be as quick to sign on the dotted line? Probably not! Yet each time you sign for a credit card, a car loan, a college loan, or anything else you are going to make payments on, you are, in essence, agreeing to be enslaved to that person or lender until that loan is paid off.

So how are you enslaved? You are enslaved through the payments (if you don't think you are enslaved to them, try not making a few), the interest (it typically starts day one), the penalties and/or late charges (these can end up being more than the interest), and all the other terms of the lender (which are in the fine print that is seldom read but *always* come to life when payments are missed). I could go on and on here. But you get the picture.

Warning Signs of the Debt Trap

Below are some warning signs that you are either caught in the debt trap or you are on your way to it. If you find yourself identifying with the warning signs below and you are already feeling some of the consequences, don't give up! I recommend a book called *Total Money Makeover* by Dave Ramsey. This resource will provide you with a complete how-to plan to get out of debt and start saving for the future.

You are unable to consistently save money.

One of the main reasons people get into debt is because they don't have any money set aside for basic emergencies, such as a flat tire, a dental cavity, an automobile deductible, broken glasses, healthcare deductibles (assuming you have insurance), a roof leak, a broken air conditioner, and—my favorite—dropping your cell phone in the toilet! If you are unable to save money for an emergency, it may be because of the debt you have accumulated through financing a car or using credit cards.

You are unable to pay your bills by the due date.

If you have a bill that is due on the first of the month and you end up having to wait until the fifteenth of the month to pay it, you are basically financing that payment for fourteen days. And it can snowball. (And I don't mean shaved ice, your favorite flavor, and a cool color!) Before you realize it, the bill you were paying on the fifteenth now has to wait until the thirtieth. At this point you may find yourself being pressured to get a payday loan or a credit card to catch up. The debt trap begins!

You find yourself having to use credit cards to pay living expenses.

How many of us think it would be a smart decision to purchase a hamburger and pay for it over eight years? Every day, young adults unconsciously make that very decision.

Many times, when people don't have enough money coming in to pay for their basic needs, they resort to using a credit card. Typically, their intention is to do this as a short-term solution and pay the credit card bill in full when it comes in. However, they soon become part of a statistic that shows you spend more money when you buy things with a credit card. This additional spending only makes things worse. The result is a maxed-out credit card and greater financial stress.

You are only able to pay the minimum amount due on your credit card.

If you have a credit card (as opposed to a debit card) and are only able to pay the minimum balance, you are financing whatever you purchased with that card. If you have a credit card balance of $1,000 with a 10 percent interest rate, it will take you approximately five years to pay your balance down to zero. (That's assuming you do not charge anything else on the card!) Change the interest rate to 18 percent, and it will take eight years to get that balance to zero.

How many of us think it would be a smart decision to purchase a hamburger and pay for it over eight years? Every day, young adults unconsciously make that very decision.

You find yourself borrowing money from your friends.
Over the last five years, almost 100 percent of the students I have worked with have answered a resounding yes when I asked if they have either borrowed money from a friend or loaned money to a friend. And a full 100 percent of those who have loaned money to a friend said that some of the money was never repaid and it caused stress in the friendship.

Why the stress? Remember Proverbs 22:7? When you loan money to a friend, that friend in essence becomes enslaved to you, the lender. I know that you may be thinking you would never treat your friend differently after lending him money. That may very well be true. However, although you may get to decide how you treat him, you don't get to decide what borrowing has made him. The Bible says he has become enslaved, and this alters the relationship until the money is repaid, no matter how you treat him.

You are spending money before you have it.
"I have a bonus coming." "I'm getting a raise at the first of the year." "I should be getting a tax refund in April." These are just a few of the reasons why people decide to purchase something today and pay for it later with money that should be coming in. No problem with that, right?

Hardly.

In a budgeting class I was teaching, I was talking about the pitfalls of spending money before you have it. Jason, a student, raised his hand and said, "I was going to purchase a laptop yesterday, but I couldn't get to the store before it closed. So I was going to purchase it today. I can finance it ninety days same as cash. I should be getting my graduation money in over the next few weeks and plan on paying the laptop off within the ninety days. What do you think?"

I told Jason that it could be God was trying to tell him something by closing the store before he got there the night before and sending him to my class the next morning! Unfortunately, he decided to proceed with his plan.

Several months later I asked him how it had worked out. Jason smiled and said, "Just like you said it would. I'm still making payments on a laptop!"

Exceptions to the Rule?

Now, I know what you may be thinking—you have to get a loan in order to purchase a car or go to college. But regardless of what you have been taught, that's not true. It may be true that you can't purchase the car you want or go to the college you want without getting a loan, but it's definitely not true that you have to get a loan. The box on the next page labeled "Graduating Without Debt" is just one example of how you could graduate from college without student debt.

One of the greatest accomplishments in your adult life will be to avoid the debt trap. Don't let college loans, credit cards, or car payments start you up the difficult path that leads to a mountain of debt!

GIVING

Although this is the last principle in this chapter, I believe it's the most important. Why? Because if you get everything else in this chapter right but get this wrong, nothing else will work the way it should.

Most of us have heard the saying "It is more blessed to give than to receive." Well, it's more than just a saying; it's truth straight from the Bible (Acts 20:35). Yet, although most people believe that the Bible instructs them to give, the percentage of people who actually give barely shows up on the radar.

Malachi 3 makes it clear that we should bring our tithe (which means 10 percent) of our income as well as offerings to the storehouse

Graduating Without Debt

Cost for Two Years at Public Community College	$5,926.00
Average Cost of Living at Home	$ -0-
Total Expenses	**$5,926.00**
Average Scholarship over Two years	-$6,000.00
Total Income	**$6,000.00**
Cost for Associate's degree	$ -0-
Income for Two Years (30 Hours Per Week)	$21,600
Summer Income for Two Years (40 Hours Per Week)	$ 9,600
Spending 50% on living expenses	$15,600
Saving 50% for undergraduate degree	$15,600
Total in Savings upon Completion of Associate's degree	**$15,600**
Room and Board for 2 Years at a 4-Year Public College	$32,000
Other Expenses (phone, books, labs, gas, etc.)	$14,700
Total Expenses	**$46,700**
Savings	$15,600
Average Scholarship	$12,000
Average Income for 2 Years (20 Hours Per Week)	$15,080
Average Summer Income for 1 Year (40 Hours Per Week)	$ 4,800
Total Income	**$47.480**
Savings (Debt) After Undergraduate Degree	**$ 780**

(our local church). It doesn't give anyone an out for being rich or poor, young or old. Here's a passage we've already looked at and now want to look at in a larger context:

> "Will a man rob God? Yet you rob me. "But you ask, 'How do we rob you?' "In tithes and offerings. You are under a curse— the whole nation of you—because you are robbing me. Bring the whole tithe into the storehouse, that there may be food in my house. Test me in this," says the LORD Almighty, "and see if I will not throw open the floodgates of heaven and pour out so much blessing that you will not have room enough for it." (Malachi 3:8-10, NIV)

Here's the bottom line: if you give the way God says, He throws open the floodgates of heaven and pours out a blessing you don't have enough room for. If you don't, you're cursed! So it's your choice: give and be blessed or don't give and be cursed.

Proverbs 11:24 (NIV) says, "One man gives freely, yet gains even more; another withholds unduly, but comes to poverty." The things you can accomplish in your life through your obedience in this area will be far greater than anything you could accomplish through keeping God's portion for yourself.

One of the greatest obstacles to being obedient in the area of giving is waiting to start. I talk to people all the time who tell me that their tithe would only be $10 per week and they just don't see how giving something that small would make a difference to their church. If you can remember this one thing, it will help you throughout your life regardless of how much or little money you make: it's not about the amount; it's about the obedience. If you aren't faithful with $10 per week, you'll never be faithful with $100 or $1,000 per week. God wants you, not your money—because when He has you, He has your money!

I encourage you to purpose in your heart right now to be obedient in bringing a tithe and an offering of everything that comes through your hands. God even says that if you are having trouble believing this, you can put Him through a test to see if it works. What you are able to do with what's left after giving will be greater than what you could have ever done by keeping it. Here is a prayer committing all your resources to God:

Dear God,

I understand that everything I have now, and will have in the future, belongs to You and that I am Your steward. I ask that You would help me to be a good steward and to manage everything You entrust to me according to Your principles, for Your purposes. Help me to not get weighted down with borrowing but to trust in You to provide everything I need in Your timing. Help me to always be obedient to give the way that Your Word has instructed me to give, and cause me to prosper so that I can accomplish Your perfect plan for my life. Amen.

Chapter 5

Your Life Plan
Robby McGee

What career have you chosen? Where are you going to college? What's your major? When are you getting married? Where are you going to live? When are you going to buy a house? Are you planning on having kids? The tsunami of questions between the ages of eighteen and twenty-two can be overwhelming! But breaking those questions down into manageable pieces may be easier than you think.

In working with students for years, Jeffrey and I have discovered that most of them are living in the moment. This is not because they want to or believe it is the best way to live; they simply have never been challenged or taught how to practically look at their life plan from a short- and long-term perspective. This chapter is intended to help you define your life dreams (dreams you want to accomplish over your lifetime), your dream goals (the major milestones that are needed to help you accomplish every life dream), and your dream steps (your action steps to start or accomplish one of your goals to help you live out one of your dreams).

The tsunami of questions between the ages of eighteen and twenty-two can be overwhelming! But breaking those questions down into manageable pieces may be easier than you think.

Although you may be creative, educated, and smart, and may have a great work ethic and top-notch relational skills, you will never reach your full potential without the ability to plan.

As the saying goes, those who fail to plan are planning to fail. Although you may be creative, educated, and smart, and may have a great work ethic and top-notch relational skills, you will never reach your full potential without the ability to plan.

Before we get too far into this chapter, however, stop for a moment and consider that God has a special purpose and plan for your life. When God sees you, He sees someone full of purpose, and there is something that He has planned for you to do that no one else can do quite like you. There is a prayer that's going to need to be prayed one day that no one can pray like you. There is something that is going to need to be said one day that no one can say like you. There is someone who is going to need to be loved one day that no one can love like you. Ephesians 2:10 (NIV) says it this way: "We are God's workmanship, created in Christ Jesus to do good works, which God prepared in advance for us to do." You are one of a kind and blessed by God to accomplish something special for Him.

The main issue at hand, however, is not how God sees you. The issue is how you see yourself. Unfortunately, many have believed untrue things that others have said about them. I hope you are not one of these people. Because, regardless of what anyone has said to you or about you, you were not an accident and you didn't catch God off guard when you were born. You are a child of purpose and God has a special plan for your life.

The first part of understanding and establishing your life plan is through the leading of God. Proverbs 29:18 (NLT) says, "When people do not accept divine guidance, they run wild. But whoever obeys the law is joyful." Similarly, Proverbs 16:9 (CEV) says, "People plan their path, but the LORD secures their steps." God is basically saying that it's our job to plan our path, and it's His job to direct us. Many students' careers, finances, and relationships have run wild because they never took the time to ask God about His guidance for their life, make a plan, and ask Him to direct their steps.

YOUR LIFE DREAMS

Life dreams are things that you would do throughout your lifetime if you had unlimited time, money, knowledge, and opportunity. Obviously none of us has unlimited resources in all of these areas, but the idea is to remove all perceived limitations and *dream big!* Think about it:

What would be your dream job? Where would you like to travel? Do you want to be married? have kids? own a house? write a book? become a public speaker or a millionaire? You get the idea.

I recently talked with a student, Chrissie, and asked her if she had written out the dreams she wanted to accomplish in her lifetime.

She said that she had not written them down, but she did have them committed to memory.

I asked her what they were.

Chrissie said, "I want to become an attorney and practice law for ten to fifteen years, get married, have kids, and seek public office or work in a ministry after practicing law."

I then asked her if she would like to own a house or if there was somewhere she wanted to travel.

Life dreams are things that you would do throughout your lifetime if you had unlimited time, money, knowledge, and opportunity.

She said, "Well, actually I would like to own two houses, one for my family and one to be used in a discipleship program for people with addictions. And I would like to travel to Israel someday." Needless to say, the more questions I asked, the bigger her dreams became.

Good for her!

Writing Your Life Dreams

Chrissie knew about the need to dream. But she still had a lot to learn about how to go after those dreams successfully. As we talked that day, she began to understand the importance of transferring her life dreams from memory to writing and then adding her goals and actions.

Hopefully you can see from Chrissie's story that writing down your dreams isn't something you should take lightly. It is something you should do thoughtfully, intentionally, and purposefully. Although there are many different ways to approach writing your life plan, below is a list of steps to help you get started with your list. (Everyone is different, so don't feel like you have to use every step in the list. Just use it as a guide.)

- Schedule a date to get away from your normal environment.
- Spend time thinking about your core values. They are the standards by which you live your life. They represent your highest priorities, most important beliefs, and most deeply held convictions.
- Before the scheduled date, pray that God would lead you and give wisdom in writing your list.
- When the day comes, remove all distractions by getting away from other people, phones, e-mail, television, videos, music, and so on.
- Begin writing a list of things you would do throughout your life if there were no limitations.
- After writing your initial list, take a walk or drive to clear your mind, pray, and reflect on what you have written down. Determine whether the list aligns with your core

values. (Make sure you have something to write or record your thoughts.)

- Refine your list based upon your time of reflection and your core values.
- Put the date on your list so that you will have a frame of reference for any future revisions. (That's right—the list doesn't have to be unchanging. It is normal for the list to change over time.)

Your list may contain only five things. Or it may contain fifty things. The important thing is to start your list. You can always add to it or take away from it as you mature and change—and most importantly, as God directs your steps because you took the time to plan!

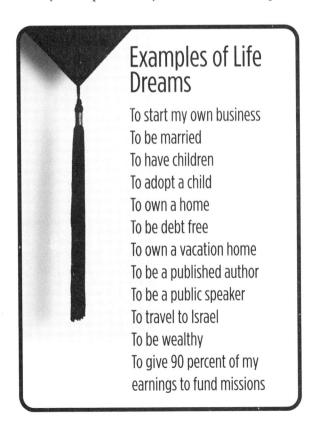

Examples of Life Dreams

To start my own business
To be married
To have children
To adopt a child
To own a home
To be debt free
To own a vacation home
To be a published author
To be a public speaker
To travel to Israel
To be wealthy
To give 90 percent of my earnings to fund missions

Once you have written down your list of dreams, you are ready to define which ones are short-term, which ones are long-term and start accomplishing them one by one.

Once you have written out your list of dreams, determine which dreams you want to start over the next three- to five-years (your short-term dreams) and which ones you want to start six or more years down the road (your long-term dreams). For instance, your dreams to start your own business, get married, purchase a home, and have children may be your short-term dreams. Being debt free, adopting a child, owning a vacation home, and traveling to Israel may fit into your category of long-term dreams.

Here are some questions to help distinguish between your short- and long-term dreams:

- Can it realistically be started or completed in three- to five-years?
- What will the end result look like?
- What, if anything, do I have to change to start or complete my dream?
- What commitments am I willing to make?

Once you have defined your life dreams you want to accomplish over the next three- to five-years, it's time to begin defining your dream goals.

Defining Your Dream Goals

Most life dreams require the accomplishment of two to three major milestones along the way. I call these milestones *dream goals*. For example, if your life dream is to own your own business, your dream goals may be to:

- graduate from college with a bachelor's degree in business administration
- intern or work for a small business owner while going to college
- start a part-time business of your own upon graduating college

So, what are the logical milestones for your dream? Clearly identify these dream goals for yourself.

Once you determine the dream goals needed to accomplish one of your life dreams, you're ready to break those goals into what I call *dream steps*.

Defining Your Dream Steps

Dream steps are the steps you are going to take in order to accomplish your goals. You will have at least one step for each goal, although it is common to have multiple steps for each goal.

Defining your dream steps usually requires some research. When defining your steps, try thinking about action words such as *learn, determine, find out, talk to, start,* and so on. Define the dream steps in small, manageable steps (and you may find it helpful to identify a start date and a completion date for at least some of them). For example, if your dream goal is to graduate from college debt free with a degree in business administration, your dream steps may be these:

- Apply for scholarships.
- Score a 30 on the ACT.
- Live at home and attend a community college for the first two years.
- Work part-time to avoid student loans.
- Attend a university after receiving your associate's degree.

And don't worry, the steps are not meant to be written in stone. It is normal to change the steps from time to time as you gain life experience, as you increase your knowledge, and most importantly as God directs!

LIVING THE DREAM

Are you ready to start living the dream? The most-asked question once someone has listed her life dreams and defined her dream goals and steps is, what now? How do I start making my dreams a reality?

The key is to do something that fits your personality. If you are outgoing and visual, you may want to create a Dream Board. If you have more of a laid-back personality, you may want to start a Dream Journal. If you are more analytical, a Dream Map may be best for you. And last but not least, if you have a driven personality, you may want to have a Dream Coach to challenge you and provide accountability to accomplish your dreams.

The Dream Board

My wife, Vanessa, is a great example of a personality that would fit dream boarding. She is an outgoing, high-energy, never-met-a-stranger kind of girl. She needs something to make her life dreams fun! A dream board works great for her because it is the perfect visual to bring her dreams to life.

A dream board is a collage of pictures from photographs, magazines, brochures, or the Internet that you either paste onto a large sheet of paper or digitally scan on the computer. If you are building a dream board, you may want to go through your pictures and magazines, or surf the Internet, and pull out pictures, words, or headlines that mean something to you. Have fun with it, making a big pile of images and phrases and words.

Next, go through the images and begin to lay your favorites on the board that most identify with your life dreams, dream goals, and dream steps. As you lay the pictures on the board, you'll get a sense of how the board should be laid out. For instance, you might assign a theme to each corner of the board, such as school, job, relationships, and spirituality. Or you may decide that you want various images to go all over the place. There's no right or wrong placement.

Then attach everything to the board and use paint or markers to add in writing wherever you want to. Some find it powerful to paste a favorite picture of themselves in the center of the board.

Last, and maybe most important, hang your dream board in a place where you will see it so that you will be reminded of your dreams often!

The Dream Journal

A dream journal is simply a blank book or a file on your computer where you write out your dreams and journal about what you are doing in order to make those dreams come to pass. For instance, if your dream is to become a published author, some of your journal entries could read like this:

- "One of my dreams is to become a published author by the age of twenty-five."
- "I am discovering that one of my passions is to help young children celebrate who God created them to be, which is what I want my first book to be about."
- "In my research I am finding that most parents compare their children to each other because they do not understand the unique personality of each of their children. My book will help to change that."
- "I wrote out the outline for my book today. It is going to have ten chapters. I have started on my first chapter, which is called 'Uniquely You,' and I plan on having the first chapter written this month!"

As you can see, your dream journal is something you write in, not only to motivate and encourage yourself, but also to hold yourself accountable and track your progress.

The Dream Map

If you are more analytical, it may be helpful for you to use a graph or chart of some kind to map out your life dream, the dream goals you need to accomplish the life dream, and the dream steps along the way. Your life dream chart may look similar to the one on the following page.

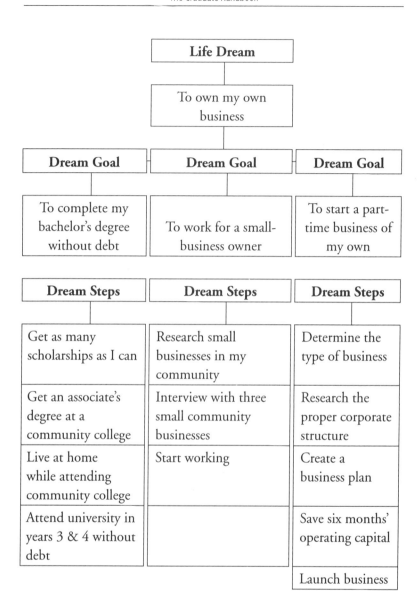

Life Dream		
To own my own business		

Dream Goal	Dream Goal	Dream Goal
To complete my bachelor's degree without debt	To work for a small-business owner	To start a part-time business of my own

Dream Steps	Dream Steps	Dream Steps
Get as many scholarships as I can	Research small businesses in my community	Determine the type of business
Get an associate's degree at a community college	Interview with three small community businesses	Research the proper corporate structure
Live at home while attending community college	Start working	Create a business plan
Attend university in years 3 & 4 without debt		Save six months' operating capital
		Launch business

There is no right or wrong way to how you organize your map or what you include. You can keep it on your computer, keep it on paper, add deadlines for your dream steps, and design it however best helps you to accomplish your life dreams!

The Dream Coach

A dream coach is someone who has more life experience than you and who will encourage, motivate, and hold you accountable to reach your life dreams. It is someone who either knows you or takes the time to get to know you and who understands the way you are wired.

Finding the right dream coach is extremely important and may take some time. Although you can hire someone to be a dream coach, at this stage of life you should be able to find someone who is willing to help you without charging. You probably have someone you trust and look up to. Consider approaching this person and sharing your dreams. Then ask if he or she would be willing to be your coach.

Your first meeting with your dream coach is typically to share your life dream list. During that meeting, your coach will help you to choose short-term dreams that you both feel can be accomplished over the next three to five years. The coach will also help you to identify your strengths and weaknesses that will either help or hinder in your attempts to achieve those dreams. Last, the coach will give you a list of dream goals and steps to reach those goals before the next time you meet. That next meeting may be two weeks or two months down the road, depending on the goals and steps you have agreed to accomplish. However, it is also common to be in touch with your coach between scheduled meetings to get advice and encouragement.

Tom Landry, the famous Dallas Cowboys football coach, once said, "A coach is someone who tells you what you don't want to hear, who has you see what you don't want to see, so you can be who you've always known you could be." Your dream coach can help you achieve your dreams and live out God's purpose and plan for your life!

A TALE OF TWO STUDENTS

Several years ago, I was teaching a college class at my church. During one semester, I taught the students many of the principles in this book, including how to develop dream goals for their life. Recently, I have had the opportunity to visit with several of the students who were in that class.

Two of them in particular stick out in my mind. If you were to meet them in a room full of people, you would think they were both great guys. However, one of them has gotten out of church, has become somewhat agnostic about God, has struggled financially, and has gone from job to job. The other one has gotten married, has three kids, is a successful business owner, and is in leadership at his church.

The difference? One of them didn't implement what had been taught, did things his way, didn't pursue wise counsel, and did not continue to learn and apply biblical principles in his life over the years. The other one did his best to implement what was being taught, continued to learn and apply biblical principles in his life, and has continually sought out wise counsel over the years.

One of them recently thanked me and told me how much he appreciated all of the principles he learned in the class. He went on to say that many of the things he had learned in those classes had helped him avoid pitfalls early on in life and provided a launching pad to start accomplishing his dreams and goals. I will let you determine which one came back to say thanks!

My hope is that one day you will be able to look back and realize that many of the principles in this book have helped you to accomplish your dreams and live the life God created you to live!

Dear God,

I know that You have a special purpose and plan for my life. I ask that You would help me to discover that purpose, to dream and make plans that enable me to accomplish what You would have me to accomplish. I know that my hope and my future are in Your hands, and I trust You to direct my steps. Help me to hear Your voice, to be obedient, and to seek out wise counsel as I strive to live out Your plan for my life. Amen.

Chapter 6

All About Interviews

Robby McGee

Once you are done with school, you will spend about one third of your life sleeping and another third working. The final third you will spend on a variety of other things, such as showering, getting dressed, eating, waiting in lines, watching TV, talking on the phone, surfing the Web, and using the restroom. (According to studies, using the restroom takes up a little over 1 percent of your time!) Since you have most likely mastered the arts of eating, sleeping, leisure, and hygiene (I'm giving you the benefit of the doubt with that last one), it seems worthwhile to focus some energy on how to be successful for something you will spend around 33 percent of your life doing—working.

You may have already had a part-time job during high school. But now that you've either graduated or are approaching graduation, you're looking ahead to entering the workforce more seriously. Does that make you say, "Yeah!" or "Yuck"?

Well, either way, know this: from God's perspective, work is a good thing. At the very beginning of history, when God told the first humans to "fill the earth and subdue it" and to "rule over" the animal kingdom, He was talking about all the kinds of work that men and women would do in making the earth a better home (Genesis 1:27-28). Did you know that Jesus was a worker—and apparently proud of it? He testified, "My Father is always at his work to this very day, and I, too, am working" (John 5:17). The apostle Paul said that people who are idle should "settle down and earn the bread they eat" because honest, hard work is to be the norm for Christ's followers (2 Thessalonians 3:12).

So congratulations on joining the ranks of the world's adult workers! Your work life has the potential to be one of the biggest contributors to your satisfaction in the decades to come.

> Remember, your job is to plan; God's is to direct your steps. If you do your part, you release God to do His.

But hey, whether you are looking to start a career right now or are just looking to earn some money for expenses, you've got to get a job first! And that almost always means going through an interview with a prospective employer. This chapter gives you practical steps on how to interview well and position yourself to be successfully employed. Remember, your job is to plan; God's is to direct your steps. If you do your part, you release God to do His. Trust me, I have interviewed many people throughout my career, and I can tell a big difference between those who have planned and those who haven't. And those who have planned well have a big advantage when it comes time to hire.

PREPARING FOR THE INTERVIEW

Imagine going in to take the test to get your driver's license without ever having driven a car.

Or running your first marathon without ever having run more than the length of a football field.

Or taking a test at school without studying. (That one might not take much imagination!)

There isn't much chance that you would think of doing any of those things without some sort of preparation. Or if you did, your attempt would likely end in failure. It will be the same if you show up for a job interview without preparing for it first.

There are basically three steps to preparing for an interview. They are to know yourself, know the company you're interested in, and know the questions you might be asked.

Know Yourself

If you have not already taken the online career assessment at www.thegraduatehandbook.com, then before reading the rest of this chapter would be the perfect time to do so. If you *have* taken the assessment, why not review it before finishing this chapter?

If there is one thing I know for certain, it is that God created you with special gifts and talents and a unique personality. Knowing those characteristics about yourself will not only help you in your business and personal relationships; it will also help you to positively impact and influence those around you. For instance, are you direct and strong willed? Optimistic, friendly, and talkative? Steady, patient, and practical? Precise and analytical? Knowing your personality type will help you to understand your greatest strengths, your greatest weaknesses, how you most effectively receive communication, how you least effectively receive communication, how you process information, what motivates you, what positive characteristics you bring to the table, and what particular career or occupation you may be best suited for.

I really wish I had known my personality type and certain occupations I was suited for when I got my first "real" job. It was a sales position at a large pawn shop in Dallas, Texas. From day one, I proved to be a below-average salesman. But my analysis of the operational structure of the store was incredible. At least I thought it was, since I was always telling my boss how it could be improved! After a few months of frustration, however, it became apparent that my boss's appreciation for my operational prowess didn't make up for my sales—or rather, lack thereof!

Had I known back then that a sales position didn't show up anywhere near the radar screen for my personality, much less on it, I could have saved him and myself much grief.

Know the Company You're Interested in Working For

It's crazy how many recent high school grads (and even older adults who ought to know better) show up for an interview without knowing much about the job they are applying for or the business where they are hoping to work. Do not make that mistake!

Before an interview, make sure you do some research on the company. This is one time when surfing the Internet for hours can be a really good thing! As you research, find out:

- What is the purpose of the organization?
- Who are their key leaders?
- What are some of their core values, their growth rate, their annual sales, and the industry trends they're dealing with?

The information you turn up about the company will help you to know for sure whether you want to work there. And I guarantee it will impress your interviewer! That's what Ashley found.

Ashley was looking for a job to take during the summer before starting college in her hometown. Her father asked her where she wanted to work.

"It doesn't really matter," she said. "Whatever I can get that pays the most, I guess."

"Well, Ashley, don't forget that you're going to be working full time all summer there—"

Ashley interrupted. "I'd like to be able to keep working there part-time after school starts too."

Her father resumed. "All the more reason to do your research and target a company you feel really good about."

Ashley thought about it and decided her dad was probably right. She went online and looked up a few of the places of business in town that she had put on her list to apply to. One quickly stood out— Chick-fil-A.

She found out that the organization's stated purpose was "to glorify God by being a faithful steward of all that is entrusted to us and to have a positive influence on all who come in contact with Chick-fil-A." Not only that, but a portion of the company's profits go to the Win-Shape Foundation, which supports a variety of Christian ministries.

All this caught her attention. Ashley had honestly never thought about the possibility that her job might contribute to advancing the Christian values she believed in.

Then Ashley read about the company's history since its founding by Truett Cathy. She learned that, from the opening of the first Chick-fil-A in the early 1960s, to pioneering the establishment of restaurants in shopping malls, to transitioning to stand-alone restaurants, drive-throughs, and licensee restaurants, Cathy has continually been a trendsetter in the industry. That's why the company has steadily grown and become the second largest quick-service restaurant chain in the United States, with more than sixteen hundred stores and more than $4 billion in sales.

Ashley liked the idea of being a part of an innovative, successful company. She was intending to be a business major, so maybe this job wouldn't just be a way to make money in the short term; maybe it could help her with her goal of being an influential businessperson.

She put in her first—and only—application at the local Chick-fil-A. The interviewer was so thrilled with her knowledge about the company and enthusiasm for working there that he hired her on the spot. Pass the grilled chicken sandwich and the waffle fries!

Know the Questions You Might Be Asked

One of the best things you can do to be prepared for an interview is to review sample questions and practice your answers by having a friend or family member ask you the questions in a mock interview. Below is a list of sample questions and responses. It should help you formulate your own answers to some of the typical questions that are asked by interviewers.

In all your answers, the key is to be honest, be positive, and be prepared.

1. "Tell me about yourself."
This is the question that is most often asked by interviewers. You need to have a short statement prepared in your mind that will outline some of your gifts and strengths and how they relate to the job you are interviewing for.

For example, if you were applying for a retail sales associate position, you could say, "I am a self-motivated individual who can work independently or fulfill an assigned role in a team environment. I love working in the retail environment and enjoy the challenge of meeting a sales goal. I have a positive, upbeat personality, and I enjoy initiating conversations with people and helping them with their needs. On a personal level, I'm single, I was born and raised on Old Hickory Lake in Hendersonville, Tennessee, and I absolutely love water sports!"

2. "Why did you leave your last job?"
Regardless of why you left your last job, you want to put it in the best possible light while remaining honest. Never speak negatively of your former management, supervisors, co-workers, or the organization. If you left your last job because you were unhappy, you might say, "I was interested in a new challenge and an opportunity to use my gifts in a different capacity than I have in the past." Or, if you have already started down a career path, you might say, "I decided that my last job wasn't going in the direction I wanted to go in my career and it was best to leave and seek new opportunities."

3. "What experience do you have in this field?"
This gives you a chance to talk about specifics that relate to the position you are applying for. If you do not have specific experience for the position, talk about your natural gifts and talents that would make you suited for the type of position you are interviewing for.

4. "What do you know about this organization?"
As mentioned under "Know the Company" above, you should take some time to research the company. You need to know some of the history, industry trends, sales and growth, their core values, and their mission statement. It also helps to know some of the key players in the organization and any special initiatives that the organization may be involved with that align with your interests.

5. *"What have you done to improve your knowledge in the last year?"*
Talk about things you have done over the past year that relate to self-improvement or the job you are applying for. Whether you attended a seminar, read a book, or achieved some sort of special certification, you need to have something you can discuss. Most interviewers want to know that personal growth and continuing education are important to you.

6. *"Are you applying for other jobs?"*
If you are applying for other jobs, just say yes. There is no need to talk about the details of your job search, such as what other companies you're applying to, unless the interviewer asks for these details. If the interviewer does push for more information, give an honest answer, whatever that is.

7. *"Why do you want to work for this organization?"*
This question is an extremely important one, so you should put some thought into it beforehand and give a sincere response based upon the research you have done on the organization. It is important that your answer not sound rehearsed but that you speak with passion and a strong understanding of what the company is and why you want to work for it.

8. *"What kind of wage or salary do you need?"*
This question can be a part of a tough little game that some interviewers want to play and that you may very well lose if you're not careful. If you give a low-ball request for a salary, you may get it even though the company was prepared to pay more. So the best advice is not to answer first but to refer the matter back to the interviewer with a response like this: "That's a hard question. Can you tell me what the wage or salary range is for the position?" The interviewer may be willing to tell you the range. But if he refuses and again presses you for a response, it is best to give a wide range.

(However, make sure the bottom number is a figure you can live with!)

9. "How long would you expect to work for us if hired?"
Although this seems like a difficult question, a simple answer will usually suffice. You can say something like "I would like for it to be a long time, as I believe the culture of your company is one that likes to retain employees and provide opportunities for advancement."

10. "Have you ever been asked to leave a position?"
If you have never been asked to leave a position, a simple no will do. However, if you have, be honest and say something like "Yes, I was asked to leave a position and would like to believe I learned something from that experience that has helped me better myself." Whatever your response is, be prepared to answer further probing, such as by explaining what you learned that helped you better yourself. Once again, you want to avoid speaking negatively about the people or organization involved.

11. "Why should we hire you?"
Point out how your assets meet what the organization needs. Do not mention any other candidates to make a comparison.

12. "What is your greatest strength?"
This is an opportunity to talk about your natural gifts and talents. As I mentioned earlier, if you have not already taken the online career assessment at www.thegraduatehandbook. com, I would recommend you take it before interviewing because it will provide you with a detailed report on your strengths and weaknesses and give you the ability, not only to provide a great response to this question, but also to understand how you can truly benefit your employer and co-workers.

13. "Why do you think you would do well at this job?"
Give several reasons and include skills, experience, and interest.

14. "Tell me about a problem you had with a supervisor."
This could be a test to see if you will speak negatively of a supervisor. If you begin to talk about a problem with a former supervisor from a negative perspective, it could have a harmful impact on the interview.

From a biblical perspective, however, the answer isn't controversial at all. The Bible is clear about the importance of submitting to authority (Ephesians 6:5-8; Colossians 3:22-25). So your reply should be something like this: "There have been times when I have disagreed with or had a problem with one of my supervisors. I believe there are always going to be problems that arise in a working environment. However, as an employee, I understand that my job is to serve those in authority over me. So, when problems or disagreements do arise with a supervisor, I believe I should go to him or her and discuss it privately and then hold those discussions in confidence."

15. "Tell me about your ability to work under pressure."
You may say that you thrive under certain types of pressure. Give an example that relates to the position you've applied for.

16. "What motivates you to do your best on the job?"
According to the book *The Five Languages of Appreciation in the Workplace,* written by Gary Chapman and Paul White, there are basically five ways that people express and receive appreciation in the workplace. They are words of affirmation, quality time, acts of service, tangible gifts, and physical touch. Every individual will be motivated by at least one of these forms of appreciation.

For those motivated by *words of appreciation,* receiving a compliment or encouragement for a specific project or task that you completed, or helped to complete, means a great deal.

If your language of appreciation is *quality time*, an affirming word may not motivate you as much as someone providing you with attention through such things as getting your input on business issues, dropping in your workspace unannounced just to see how things are going, or going to lunch and having an uninterrupted quality conversation.

Those whose have *act of service* as their language of appreciation enjoy chipping in to help others complete a task. Also, it could make a huge impression on them when someone takes the time to come alongside them and lend a hand.

If your language of appreciation is *tangible gifts*, you feel most appreciated when someone provides you with something you value. For instance, someone finding what restaurant you most enjoy and giving you a gift card. Or finding out your favorite band and getting tickets to a concert.

According to *The Five Languages of Appreciation in the Workplace,* physical touch is the most challenging language of appreciation to use appropriately in the workplace. Some of the authors' recommendations include giving a compliment while at the same time offering a firm handshake, a pat on the back, or a high-five.

So if your language of appreciation is acts of service, the answer to "What motivates you to do your best on the job?" could be this: "First, I believe knowing that what I am doing is important to helping the company achieve its goals is very motivating. The second thing would be having the right tools to do the job. And third, I'm really motivated by teamwork, such as having the chance to help someone else once my work is caught up, or when someone helps me when extenuating circumstances come up that may require some extra help."

17. "Are you willing to work overtime? Nights? Weekends?"
Again, be honest. If you have limitations that keep you from working certain hours, or if you are simply not willing to

work nights, weekends, or overtime for a long period of time, just say so. It will save you and your employer a lot of frustration in the future.

18. *"What's your biggest weakness?"*

If you say you don't have a weakness, you're obviously lying. So be prepared to share at least one weakness. But do it in a way that isn't too destructive to your own chances for getting the job. For example, your reply to this question could be "In my current job I've been told that I occasionally focus too much on the details and miss the bigger picture, so I've been spending time laying out the complete project every day to keep track of my overall progress."

19. *The random question*

Don't be surprised if a random question is thrown in the mix, such as "Why are manhole covers round?" or "If you could be any superhero, who would it be?" There's isn't typically a right or wrong answer to this kind of question; it's either used as an icebreaker or the interviewer just wants to see how you think on your feet. Have some fun with it—but not *too much* fun!

20. *"Do you have any questions for me?"*

You always need to have questions prepared for the interviewer. Below is a sample of questions for you to choose from:

- "What are the most difficult issues now facing the organization?"
- "Can you describe the organizational structure?"
- "What new services or products, if any, is the organization planning?"
- "What is the first matter that needs to be addressed in this position?"

- "Who are the major competitors in the area?"
- "How have the responsibilities for the position been performed in the past?"
- "How does the organization measure performance?"
- "Is there anything unique about the position?"

THE INTERVIEW

Studies have indicated that the interviewer makes his or her first judg-

ment of you within ten seconds of the interview and then makes the decision not to hire within five to fifteen minutes. Within that short time frame, the interviewer determines the answers to key questions like these: *Do I like him? Do I trust this person? Is she personable?* The interviewer then spends the rest of the time supporting that decision. Presenting yourself poorly during those first few minutes will make it almost impossible to recover.

Fortunately, there are things you can do to make a good impression in the interview from start to finish.

Know the Time and Place

I know this seems elementary, but you would be surprised by how many people show up late for an interview because they didn't know the exact time or location for it. Many a job candidate has been denied an interview and sent home because he or she was late for the scheduled interview time.

If possible, you should get the time and location of the interview in an

Studies have indicated that the interviewer makes his or her first judgment of you within ten seconds of the interview and then makes the decision not to hire within five to fifteen minutes.

e-mail or some other form that can be confirmed. That way, if there is ever any confusion, you have something to refer back to.

If you are familiar with where you are going, you should plan on arriving at the location thirty minutes before your scheduled interview time. This will give you time to relax and clear your thoughts for the interview. However, you should wait to go and check in for your interview until five or ten minutes before your scheduled interview time.

If you are not familiar with the area where you are going to interview, it is a good idea to do a dry run to the location a day or two before your interview.

Also, if possible, it is best to schedule late-morning appointments, usually 10:00 or 11:00 a.m. Why? Scheduling too early may not allow the interviewer to get her day started (or have his first cup of coffee), and scheduling after lunch or too late in the day can subject you to the after-lunch carb overload or the mountain of distractions that may have accumulated throughout the day.

Last, make sure you know the name and title of the interviewer. However, do not use his or her first name unless you are asked to.

Know What to Bring

Bring some sort of portfolio or small case and carry extra copies of your résumé, a list of references, a note pad, and a pen. It is best to leave your cell phone and any other electronic devices in the car or keep them turned off.

Know How to Dress

Dress appropriately for the interview. Most of the time, you should dress conservatively. For men, that may be a suit, khakis, or slacks and a dress shirt. For women, that would be professional-looking clothes, not the newest trendy looks. Remember, it's not the time to make a fashion statement. Also, it is best not to wear perfume or cologne, since your interviewer may find your favorite fragrance offensive. (One interviewer rejected a job applicant because she was wearing the same perfume his ex-wife used!) Finally, avoid extreme hairstyles or colors, keep your shoes moderate, do not wear excessive jewelry, don't chew gum, and don't bring in drinks or snacks. And by all means, take a breath mint!

Know How to Make a Good Impression

Focus on being up! When you walk into the room, keep your head up shoulders back, stand up straight, make eye contact (poor eye contact shows a lack of confidence), firmly shake the interviewer's hand (a limp handshake can be seen as a sign of weakness), and greet the interviewer by name and title (Mr. or Ms.).

The interviewer will typically ask you to have a seat. When you are sitting down, be aware of your body language. Most people will lean forward slightly when they are interested in what someone is saying. Leaning back slightly can show knowledge and confidence. But slouching down and crossing your arms can make you seem close-minded or disengaged from a conversation. Also, do your best not to fidget or constantly move around in your chair, since this can be interpreted as being nervous or insecure.

The interviewer will probably try to warm up the conversation by starting off with some small talk. He or she may talk about a hobby mentioned on your résumé or ask where you're from. Usually the interviewer is doing this to try to make you comfortable. Remember, however, that you are still being interviewed during the small talk.

You should also make sure that you speak respectfully by saying "Yes sir (or ma'am)," "Thank you," "Please," and "You're welcome" and by using proper English rather than slang terms.

Also, be aware of any personal habits that may be annoying or distracting during the interview, such as twirling your hair, tapping on the table, bouncing your legs, or snorting when you laugh.

Last, don't be uncomfortable with silence. Some interviewers may purposefully use silence to see how you respond. If the interviewer falls silent, just pleasantly maintain eye contact and wait for him or her to proceed.

Know How to Exit the Interview

In closing, summarize your qualifications and show the interviewer that you have listened and heard what he or she has said about the position and company. Also, ask the interviewer for a business card. This will ensure that you have the proper title, name, and address to send a thank-you card.

As you leave, make sure that you look the interviewer in the eye, firmly shake hands, and ask him or her what the next step in the

Top 20 Interview Busters

1. Poor personal appearance
2. A know-it-all attitude
3. A cell phone ringing
4. Misleading or outright lying on a résumé
5. Inability to express oneself clearly
6. Lack of knowledge of the career field
7. Questionable conduct on social networking sites
8. Poor handling of personal finances
9. Lack of interest or enthusiasm
10. Expressing an unhappy attitude
11. Lack of confidence and poise
12. Overemphasis on the pay
13. Dropping names in an effort to impress the interviewer
14. Lack of tact, courtesy, or maturity
15. Being late to the interview
16. An indefinite response to questions
17. Condemnation of past employers
18. Asking no questions about the position
19. Poor knowledge of the company
20. Failure to express appreciation for interviewer's time

process is. You might say, "When can I expect a decision to be made?" or "Is there a certain day when I may call back?"

Make sure that you send the thank-you card letting the interviewer know that you appreciate him or her taking time to allow you to interview. Send this card either the day of or the day after the interview.

YOUR SOURCE OF CONFIDENCE

I recently read a story about a young man who was interviewing at a bank for his first job after graduating from college. When his interviewer asked him to describe a stressful situation at a previous job, he started telling them about his summer job, which was selling driving lessons. The interviewer listened carefully to the young man's answer and followed up with the question "What did you do to alleviate this stress?" His knee-jerk reaction was to say something sarcastic. So he paused for a split second, shrugged his shoulders, and replied, "I drank heavily." The young man did not get the job!

This chapter is designed to help you avoid making a mistake like the one this man made. If you will plan for your interview by taking the time to know yourself, know the company, and know the questions, you will have done your part and have the confidence to interview well. After that, it's up to God to do His part—which is a really safe place for you to be!

Consider the prayer below any time you are launching out to the wonderful world of interviews.

Dear God,
Thank You for the gift of work that You created in the beginning to bring provision and fulfillment into my life. I thank You for the gifts, talents, and personality that You have blessed me with for the purpose of bringing Your kingdom and Your will upon this earth. Give me the wisdom, knowledge, guidance, and understanding to interview well and to find a place of employment where my gifts, talents, and life can be used for Your glory. Amen.

Chapter 7

Who Wants to Be a Millionaire?

Robby McGee

Every time I ask the question "Who wants to be a millionaire?" the answer is almost always unanimous: "I do! I do! I do!" Not really surprising, is it?

But it gets interesting when I ask a follow-up question: "Why?" This time the answers are slower to come and tend to be all over the board. Some say they'd like to be wealthy so they can have a nice house or car. Some say it's because they want to travel or start their own business. Some mention that rich people have a lot of friends. And every now and then I come across someone who says he or she wants to use wealth to help others.

So now let me turn it around to you: Would you like to be a millionaire? Why?

The good news is, you don't have to go on a game show, win the lottery, or strike it rich with a one-of-a-kind idea to become a millionaire. The fact is, just about everyone reading this chapter has the potential to retire a millionaire. And over the next few pages I'm going to be giving you solid, tested advice about how to get there.

But before we talk about the *how* of obtaining wealth, we need to look more closely at the *why*.

HEART FIRST

The Bible has a lot to say about the benefits of being wealthy, but it also contains many warnings about the pitfalls surrounding wealth. On the benefits side, Proverbs 10:22 (NIV) says, "The blessing of the LORD brings wealth, and he adds no trouble to it." And it's interesting to note

> The truth is, wealth itself is never an issue with God; it is the person's heart, along with what that person does with the wealth, that is at issue.

in Matthew 27:57-60 that it was a rich follower of Jesus who provided for the burial of Jesus. Sounds good so far, right? But wait—there are also some verses that ought to make us pause to think. Proverbs 11:28 (NIV) says, "Whoever trusts in his riches will fall, but the righteous will thrive like a green leaf." *Hmm.* And then, even more soberingly, in Matthew 19:23 (NIV) we read these words of Jesus: "I tell you the truth, it is hard for a rich man to enter the kingdom of heaven."

So, where does all this leave us?

The truth is, wealth itself is never an issue with God; it is the person's heart, along with what that person does with the wealth, that is at issue. Some verses can help us see this distinction. For example, Luke 16:13 (NIV) says, "No servant can serve two masters. Either he will hate the one and love the other, or he will be devoted to the one and despise the other. You cannot serve both God and Money." And 2 Corinthians 9:11 (NIV) says, "You will be made rich in every way so that you can be generous on every occasion, and through us your generosity will result in thanksgiving to God."

When you understand that a plan to obtain wealth is simply a tool that releases God's direction in how you live and how you give, it helps you to make saving and investing the right kind of priority in your life. Remember, no matter how much or how little money we accumulate in a lifetime, it all belongs to God. We are just managers of *His* wealth!

I have learned that it's easy to say that it all belongs to God…until He asks for a big part of it. Fortunately, my first experience with this reality came fairly early in life.

My wife, Vanessa, and I were a young married couple. If you had asked me at that time if we were faithful in giving, I would have said, "Absolutely!" But then our church started teaching on stewardship. For the first time in our lives, we weren't being challenged with an amount to give; we were being challenged to pray about how much to give and then be obedient to whatever God was telling us to do. Gradually, as I sat through lesson after lesson about stewardship, I came to the realization that we had never spent much time asking God what He wanted us to give. So Vanessa and I agreed that we needed to do this.

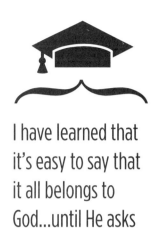

I have learned that it's easy to say that it all belongs to God...until He asks for a big part of it.

As we began to pray, I felt like God was leading me to an amount that we were to give. And I have to admit, I thought it was a little much! So, instead of immediately giving in, I decided to ask God to confirm the amount with Vanessa.

One night we sat down at our dining room table, and I brought with me two pens and two pieces of paper. I said to Vanessa, "I want you to write down the amount you feel that God has given you for what we are supposed to give. I'll write down the amount I feel like God has given me. Okay?"

She agreed. And with a little trepidation in our hearts, we wrote down our figures. Then we laid our pieces of paper on the table, writing side down.

I said, "All right, let's turn our pieces of paper over at the same time."

Have you guessed it? When we turned our pieces of paper over, we saw that both of them named the exact same dollar figure! You should have seen the expressions on our faces. God *had* been speaking to us about our giving!

The exact figure we came up with that night doesn't matter. What matters was that we now knew how we needed to be obedient to God. We made a three-year commitment to give what God had asked for, and in order to fulfill that commitment, we worked out some changes in our life. These changes weren't easy, especially at first. But I can tell you that at the end of that three-year period, the changes we made in order to be obedient changed our lives forever. I think for the first time in my life God truly had His rightful place over any amount of money or any possession we had. Since that day, it's incredible what God has allowed us to be a part of and what He's allowed us to help accomplish in His Kingdom.

So here's my strong advice: Before you pursue wealth, make sure your heart is right. Make sure you're going after that million dollars (or more), not to satisfy selfish desires that you come up with on your own, but to better live the life God is calling you to. For the children of God, earthly prosperity always has a heavenly purpose.

FOUR STEPS TO A MILLION DOLLARS

Once you understand the purpose of wealth, the next question is, are you willing to do what it takes to acquire that wealth? This means deferring gratification while you're on the path to the wealth you seek. And deferring gratification is not something that many people in our society are good at.

Money management guru Dave Ramsey says, "You have to live like no one else now so that later you can live like no one else." If you want to drive like no one else later, you have to drive like no one else now, which means you drive a vehicle you can pay cash for instead of financing one and making a car payment. If you want to vacation like no one else later, you have to vacation like no one else now, which means you may have to enjoy a "staycation" in which you hang out close to home instead of traveling to some vacation destination. You get the idea.

Not a thrilling prospect to you? Well, don't ignore the payoff. If you will live like no one else now—that is, starting while you are still in your teens or early twenties—you will get to live your life like no one else later…and a lot sooner!

This chapter shares four basic steps to obtaining millionaire status:

- Avoid borrowing.
- Start saving today.
- Save consistently.
- Invest your savings wisely.

That's it—pretty simple stuff. Sure, I could give you a more complicated formula with fancy terminology that would sound much more impressive. My goal, however, is not to impress you. My goal is to help you see how basic financial principles can make financial success possible...for *you*!

Step 1: Avoid Borrowing

Although we touch on the importance of not borrowing in the "Money Game" chapter, here I want to show you the saving/investment benefits of not borrowing. The truth is, once you start borrowing and go into debt, it starts a vicious cycle that keeps you from being able to save money, which is one of the basic steps to obtaining your millionaire status.

Let's take a look at a financial decision that many high school and college graduates make year after year, as well as the unforeseen results of that decision. What's the decision? To finance a new or slightly used car. Consider this: currently the average car payment on a new car is between $350 and $500 per month, depending on the price of the car, the length of time financed, and the interest. However, most people who purchase that new car never see the long-term results of that purchase, nor are they shown the benefits of purchasing an older car and starting a saving/investment plan. So let's look at two very different financial outcomes based upon two very different financial choices, both of which provided a car.

For her twentieth birthday, Jana decided to buy a brand-new car. She made monthly payments on her new car and paid it off in five years. Although she now owned the car with no more payments, she was getting a little tired of driving the same old car, so she decided to trade it in and purchase another brand-new car. She went to the dealership, traded in her old car, and financed the new car for another five years. She continued to do this every five years until her sixty-fifth birthday.

On the other hand, on Justin's twentieth birthday, he decided that he was going to continue to drive his existing car for another five years. He also decided that he was going to take the money he would have been spending on a new car and invest it instead. Then, on his twenty-fifth birthday, Justin decided to celebrate by selling (or trad-

TABLE 1

Years	New Car Cost *	Trade-In **	Amount Financed	Monthly Payment ***	Annual Payment	Total Spent Every 5 years
1-5	$24,000.00	$ -	$ 24,000.00	$ 475.00	$ 5,700.00	$ 28,500.00
6-10	$25,980.00	$12,000.00	$ 13,980.00	$ 276.82	$ 3,321.84	$ 16,609.20
11-15	$28,115.00	$12,990.00	$ 15,125.00	$ 299.49	$ 3,593.88	$ 17,969.40
16-20	$30,435.00	$14,057.50	$ 16,377.50	$ 324.29	$ 3,891.48	$ 19,457.40
21-25	$32,945.00	$15,217.50	$ 17,727.50	$ 351.03	$ 4,212.36	$ 21,061.80
26-30	$35,660.00	$16,472.50	$ 19,187.50	$ 379.94	$ 4,559.28	$ 22,796.40
31-35	$38,600.00	$17,830.00	$ 20,770.00	$ 411.27	$ 4,935.24	$ 24,676.20
36-40	$41,785.00	$19,300.00	$ 22,485.00	$ 445.23	$ 5,342.76	$ 26,713.80
41-45	$45,230.00	$20,892.50	$ 24,337.50	$ 481.91	$ 5,782.92	$ 28,914.60
					Total Spent	$ 206,698.80

* Assumes 3% inflation per year
** Assumes 50% depreciation over a 5 year period
*** Assumes the trade-in value was applied to new car purchase to lower payment

TABLE 2

Years	Used Car Cost *	Trade-In **	Interest Earned ***	Monthly Savings	Annual Savings	Total Saved Every 5 Years
1-5	$ -	$ -	$ 5,704.99	$ 475.00	$ 5,700.00	$ 34,204.99
6-10	$12,000.00	$ -	$ 12,598.11	$ 276.82	$ 3,321.84	$ 51,412.30
11-15	$12,990.00	$ 6,495.00	$ 19,643.16	$ 299.49	$ 3,593.88	$ 82,529.86
16-20	$14,057.50	$ 7,028.75	$ 29,778.18	$ 324.29	$ 3,891.48	$ 104,184.19
21-25	$15,217.50	$ 7,608.75	$ 44,306.15	$ 351.03	$ 4,212.36	$ 153,754.64
26-30	$16,472.50	$ 8,236.25	$ 65,073.58	$ 379.94	$ 4,559.28	$ 224,524.62
31-35	$17,830.00	$ 8,915.00	$ 94,700.07	$ 411.27	$ 4,935.24	$ 325,392.14
36-40	$19,300.00	$ 9,650.00	$136,902.48	$ 445.23	$ 5,342.76	$ 468,973.42
41-45	$20,892.50	$ -	$196,947.99	$ 481.91	$ 5,782.92	$ 673,147.26
					Total Saved	$ 673,147.26

* Assumes purchasing 5 year old vehicle at 50% depreciation
** Assumes 50% depreciation over a 5 year period
*** Assumes earning 7% on your investment

ing in) his old car and purchasing a five-year-old used car (possibly the one Jana was trading in). He purchased the car with the money he had received from selling his old car and a portion of the cash he had been investing.

Would this one choice really make that big of a difference between Jana and Justin in the long run? Just take a look! Table 1 shows Jana's results, while Table 2 shows Justin's results.

As you can see, at the end of forty-five years, Jana has a car valued at approximately $22,500 and zero savings. On the other hand, although Justin's car is only worth $11,000, he has almost $675,000 in savings! This step alone would take Justin on two-thirds of his journey to becoming a millionaire. As for Jana, unless she saved in other areas, her greatest hope is that she married Justin!

Step 2: Start Saving Today, Not Tomorrow

When people ask me when the best time is to start saving, my answer is always the same: *today!* Proverbs 21:20 (NIV) says, "In the house of the wise are stores of choice food and oil, but a foolish man devours all he has." This is as true today as ever.

A lot of people spend everything they earn on "stuff." They use excuses such as "I will start saving money when I get a raise," or "...when I get my car paid off," or "...when I get my student loans paid off." (I could fill up a page or two with all the excuses I have heard!) But they usually look up one day and realize that they are past their prime earning years with little or no money saved up and are facing a retirement of barely getting by (or are forced to postpone retirement for several years).

I know the idea of retirement may seem silly to you today, particularly if

When people ask me when the best time is to start saving, my answer is always the same: **today!**

you are in your final year of high school and are just trying to pass Algebra 2 so you can graduate. But, again, planning is important to success. Making up your mind now to *not* be one of these people will be a choice you will never regret!

But there's an interesting question here. Why do people find it so hard to start saving? Answer: They just don't see it as important. And the reason for this is misplaced priorities.

I believe most of us can agree that retailers of every type are continually bombarding us with advertisements that make a product look like a critical need as opposed to an emotional want. These advertisements are designed to make us believe that frequenting the newest restaurant, or buying the latest clothes, phone, or computer, is something we must do in order to live a life of contentment.

Jeffrey admits to me that he has to fight the urge not to go and stand in line at his favorite computer store ever time they release a new product. As I was writing this chapter, he said, "Determination and discipline are critical to denying yourself the pleasures of buying stuff you think you need." I agree. I have learned that true contentment is less about having the latest and the newest stuff and more about having the resources to do whatever God wants you to do whenever He wants you to do it.

Perhaps you're thinking, *This all sounds good, but there is no way I could start saving money today.* Well, let's consider an example that may help you look at your situation differently.

Let's say you went to the hospital this week and the doctor told you that you have a rare disease for which you need treatments that your insurance would not cover. He said that unless you had surgery within the next twelve months—a surgery that would cost you $2,400—you were going to die. Would you forgo buying new clothes, getting the latest technology gadget, going out to eat, or anything else that would get in the way of your saving that $2,400? You bet you would! All of the sudden, saving would become a priority.

Although that may be an extreme example, it shows us that there are different ways of looking at the value of saving. In real life, there are thousands of people every year who retire wishing they could start over, go back to their youth, give up most of the stuff they accumulated, and save. How cool it is to know that you have the opportunity to do that today!

Let's say you started a saving/investment plan right after high school graduation. As you will see, it does not take a lot of money to have big results. Just follow these four simple steps:

- Save $500 out of the money your friends and relatives send you for graduating (make sure to send out plenty of graduation invitations!).
- Save $365 per year (a dollar a day) during your four years of college.
- Save $1,200 per year ($100 per month) for the next six years.
- Save $6,000 per year ($500 per month) until age sixty-seven.

As you can see below, you will have accumulated $2,577,021 by the time you turn sixty-seven years old. And if you could somehow grow your money at 12 percent return (difficult but not necessarily impossible), your savings would have grown to a whopping $6,802,870!

TABLE 3.

Age	Savings	Interest	Total
18-21	$1,960.00	$0.00	$ 1,960.00
22-27	$7,200.00	$3,768.57	$ 10,968.57
28-66	$234,000.00	$2,330,092.96	$ 2,564,092.96
		Age 67	**$ 2,577,021.53**

Step 3: Save Consistently

One of the greatest mistakes you can make in accumulating wealth is inconsistency. Many individuals stop saving based upon the state of the economy or life circumstances. Yet inconsistency can devastate two of the most powerful financial keys you can put to work in your life: compound interest and dollar-cost averaging. These two keys provide some of the greatest opportunities for those who are willing to implement a savings plan and stay consistent.

The first key—compound interest—is one of the most powerful financial forces on the face of the earth…and it's available to everyone, regardless of financial knowledge! But since many people confuse *simple interest* with *compound interest*, it may be helpful to give a quick illustration of the difference between the two.

We'll assume you invested $1,000 at a bank earning a 10 percent annual fixed-interest rate for twenty years. A simple-interest calculation on the $1,000 would take 10 percent per year on $1,000, which is $100 per year, and multiply it by twenty years, which would give you $2,000 ($100 per year of earned interest x 20 years). A compound-interest calculation would take the $100 of interest màde in the first year, add it to the original $1,000 investment at the end of the year, and calculate interest in the second year on $1,100, not $1,000. That means your interest in the second year would be $110 (10 percent of the $1,100). In the first few years, the difference is not particularly obvious. But after twenty years the amount of interest earned would be $5,728 instead of $2,000!

To really understand the impact of consistency and compound interest, let's go back and use Table 3 as an example. If you decided to stop saving and investing between years five through ten as outlined in Table 3, during that time you would miss out on $12,099 ($7,200 of savings and the compounding interest of $4,899). In the short term, that doesn't seem like a huge amount. But think about this: even if you picked up the Table 3 savings plan in year eleven and continued consistently with it until you were sixty-seven years old, your total at retirement would be $2,214,915. That means the inconsistency and diminished compound interest between years five through ten would cost you over $362,000 by age sixty-seven! As you can see, saving consistently with compound interest really pays off.

The second key to wealth accumulation over time—dollar-cost averaging—works like this. Let's say you have started your saving/investing plan and everything is going great. However, the economy starts to take a downturn and you see the savings you have invested going down in value. Out of fear, you stop investing until the value goes back up. In this scenario, you would have just missed out on the benefits of what is called *dollar-cost averaging*. The term probably sounds more complicated than it is. Simply put, it is buying a fixed dollar amount of an investment on a regular schedule, regardless of the share price.

As with much of my advice in this book, I learned the lesson of dollar-cost averaging the hard way. When I was thirty-five years old, I sold a house and made a nice profit. I took that money and invested it in mutual funds. The first couple of months were great. I watched my investments go up over $10,000! However, over the next few months, I watched my investment go from a $10,000 gain to a loss of $30,000. I panicked and sold all the mutual fund shares I had purchased. Less than a year later, those same mutual funds had gone back up over $35,000 in value. That's right: if I had not cashed out my investment, I not only would not have lost $30,000; I would have made an additional $5,000. And if I had continued investing when my mutual fund shares declined (which is the principle of dollar-cost averaging), my gains would have increased by over 30 percent!

Here's a simple example of how it works and the potential benefits. Let's say you buy one share of X stock for $10 and then X stock falls in value by 50 percent. That would mean X stock, which you paid $10 for, would now be worth $5. If you continue consistently investing according to your plan, however, you would buy another $10 worth of X stock. Since X stock is now selling for $5 per share, you would be buying two shares of X stock for your $10. This means you would now own three shares of X stock for which you paid $20. To get your dollar-cost average per share, you simply divide your total investment by your number of shares ($20 ÷ 3 = $6.67). This means your dollar-cost average per share is now $6.67. When X stock goes back up to $10 per share, your three shares of X stock will be worth $30 (which is 50 percent more than your dollar-cost average per share). In this example, if you had decided to hold on to your $10 instead of consistently sticking with your investing plan, you would have lost out on a 50 percent return.

Investing is for everyone, and the earlier you start investing, the less money it will take to become a millionaire!

I know firsthand both the negative consequences and the benefits of a consistent saving/investing plan, as I have experienced both. Believe me, it's easy to find an excuse for not sticking with a saving/investing plan. *I need the money for vacation. The economy is bad. The new school year is starting. There's a great sale. It's Christmas. A special birthday or anniversary is coming up.* But if you will say no to these excuses, sticking with your plan can provide you with great blessings in the future!

Step 4: Invest Wisely

How do I start investing? Should I invest in single stocks? Bonds? Mutual funds? Gold? Exchange-traded funds? Real estate? My own business? Or what?

You may have never made a long-term investment and may think investing is only for the rich. So let's clear up the myth right now: investing is for everyone, and the earlier you start investing, the less money it will take to become a millionaire!

What are the most common types of investments?
Even if you plan on using a broker to help with your investments, it pays to know about the most common types of investments, which are stocks, bonds, ETFs, and mutual funds. As you may find out, there are many different opinions about what to invest in. Some consider single stocks an excellent long-term investment, while others stay away from single stocks and only invest in bonds, ETFs, mutual funds, or real estate.

Here are simple definitions of four of the most common types of investments.

- *Single stocks* are basically pieces of ownership in a company that are sold in shares. Every shareholder owns a piece of the company, participating in the gains and losses of the company stock when the stock price goes up or down.

- A *bond* is a debt security, similar to an IOU or a loan. When you purchase a bond, you are actually lending money to a government, municipality, corporation, federal agency, or other entity known as an *issuer*. In return for the money you are lending, the issuer provides you with a bond that promises to pay you, the investor, a specified rate of interest during the life of the bond and to repay you the face value of the bond (the principal) when it *matures*, or comes due.

- A *mutual fund* is a professionally managed investment consisting of a portfolio of stocks, bonds, and other securities. Investing in a mutual fund allows you to achieve diversity in your investment portfolio without having to purchase single stocks in multiple companies.

- An *exchange-traded fund* (ETF) is an investment fund traded on stock exchanges, much like stocks. Similar to a mutual fund, however, an ETF holds multiple assets such as stocks, commodities, or bonds. Most ETFs track an index (an index groups together a certain list of stocks and takes an average of their prices to represent the overall market performance of a certain sector). For instance, if you wanted to invest in the S&P 500 ETF, which is an index that tracks five hundred of the largest, mostly widely held companies, you would purchase shares of an ETF with the acronym SPY. Some of the most common indexes are the Dow Jones, the S&P 500, and the Russell 3000. ETFs may be attractive as investments because of their diversity and stocklike trading features.

For someone who is just beginning to invest, it would be virtually impossible to purchase all the individual stocks and bonds needed to create a balanced portfolio. Therefore, if you are just getting started as an investor, I believe mutual funds and ETFs are the way to go.

How do I choose a broker or brokerage firm?

To buy and sell stocks, bonds, ETFs and mutual funds, you need to have an account with a broker or brokerage firm. The most basic function of a broker is to execute trades for you, the investor. But many brokers offer additional services, such as investment advice and portfolio management.

In the past, there have basically been two different kinds of brokerage services, the discount broker and the full-service broker. The *discount broker* is typically an online brokerage service that only executes a trade. You, as the investor, fill out the details of the trade on the website, then hit the Buy or Sell button, and the online broker makes the trade. Discount brokers may charge as little as $5 to $20 per trade. The *full-service broker*, on the other hand, should do much more than just execute trades. Such brokers are professional money managers and planners who work with a client to develop a strategy and maintain his or her portfolio according to that strategy. But because of the custom strategy and personalized service, the commissions and additional fees from a full-service broker may be as much as ten to fifteen times that of the discount broker.

The good news is that the ease and low cost of online discount broker investing has created a new generation of online brokers. These *online brokers* are great for young investors who are just getting started because they fill the investment advice vacuum between the online discount broker and the traditional full-service broker. You may pay between $15 and $30 per trade, but you'll get more guidance and support than from a traditional online discount broker.

As a beginning investor, you may find it difficult to choose between a discount broker and a full-service broker. Although discount brokers are inexpensive, using one of them leaves you on your own in deciding what to invest in. On the other hand, the higher commissions charged by the full-service broker can be impractical for the young first-time investor. That's why I believe that one of the new-generation online brokers may be your best option to get started.

PROSPERITY AND GOD'S PLAN

Phillip is a man I've known for years, and I've watched as he's lived out many of the principles in this chapter.

From the time Phillip started working as a teenager, he committed himself to being a giver. Beyond his tithe, Phillip budgeted an additional percentage of his income to set aside specifically for giving to ministries and people in need. Starting early made it easy to live with a smaller portion of his income, even when money was tight. In his early twenties, Phillip learned more about the importance of saving, and he continued his discipline of living well within his means so that he could continue to be a giver and set aside savings as well.

God's blessing on Phillip's faithfulness has been incredible. As his income has increased, so has his giving and saving. Today, in his mid thirties, he is the owner of a successful business, has investments in real estate and mutual funds, and each year is able to give away several times what he earned in his early twenties. He is also well on his way to becoming a millionaire by age fifty-five. His life dream—one that once seemed extravagant but now seems well within his reach—is to eventually give away at least 50 percent of his income every year!

Jeremiah 29:11 (NIV, emphasis added) says, " 'I know the plans I have for you,' declares the LORD, 'plans to *prosper* you and not to harm you, plans to give you hope and a future.' " I pray this chapter helps you to understand that God wants you to prosper and that His plan is to give you hope and a future. If you can get that, you can begin to realize that wealth is just a tool to help bring that hope and that future into being and to release God's direction for your life.

Dear God,

I believe that You not only supply all of my needs; I believe that You want to prosper me and give me a hope and a future so that I can give as You direct me to give in order to be a blessing to others. Help me to never allow money to master me and control my life, but to remember that everything belongs to You and I am Your steward. Give me wisdom to save and make wise financial decisions now so that I will have the resources I need to live out Your giving plan for my life. Amen.

Chapter 8

College Life
Jeffrey Dean

I vividly remember two things about my first day of college. First, I was excited! Second, I was crazy nervous!

Up until that point of my life, I hadn't experienced anything more exciting than my first day on a college campus of more than four thousand people. None of whom I knew. In a new city. Away from my parents. With freedom to make my own choices and no one to tell me what to do.

And up until that point of my life, I hadn't experienced anything more frightening than my first day on a college campus of more than four thousand people. None of whom I knew. In a new city. Away from my parents. With freedom to make my own choices and no one to tell me what to do.

The transition from high school to college raises a mix of emotions. On the one hand, who wouldn't be excited about the chance to finally graduate high school, move out of the house, and begin an entirely new season of life? Freshman year almost always equates to new friends, new clothes, a new environment, and just about a new everything. The flip side, of course, is that there most likely will no longer be anyone there to have a hot breakfast ready for you as you race out of the house in the morning, have the fridge stocked with your favorite after-school snacks, or have your favorite jeans washed and ready for another Friday night of high school fun. Not to mention the fact that you are now spending the next ten months of your life sharing a room about the size of your parents' walk-in closet with someone you barely know.

College life. There's nothing like it. Half the fun is the unknown of what is to come.

It is impossible to learn everything there is to know about college life in this one chapter. But as we've said over and over again in this book, if you plan, God will direct. I've included in this chapter everything I wish someone would have told me to help me be the most prepared I could have been as I began my college career.

WEEK–ONE JITTERS ARE NORMAL

No matter how independent you are, when your parents drive off and leave you standing there on your college campus the first day, it can be intimidating. The hectic pace of getting your dorm room in order, figuring out your class schedule, getting to know your roommate, scoping out the campus, and discerning the business school from the humanities school can be overwhelming. I remember this well.

Just know that the first week or two of school will most likely be fun, exciting, intimidating, and scary. All of this is a part of transition from high school to the rest of your life.

On my first day, I found out I was rooming with a baseball player from Lawrenceburg, Tennessee. The first thing he said to me was "Hey. I'm Kevin. You don't mind if I chew in here, do you?" The fact that I thought he was referring to Bubble Yum explains a lot about our differences.

I spent the first few nights trying to get used to the smell of saliva-soaked tobacco in our room. I'll never forget one night that first week when I got out of bed for a trip to the boys' room and tripped over one of Kevin's many cups of Copenhagen spit he had sitting around the room. (Unless that carpet has been replaced in our old dorm room, I wouldn't be surprised if that stain were still there.)

Kevin and I roomed together only one semester. But we became really good friends and taught each other things about ourselves we didn't even know.

I loved college. If you choose to go to college, I hope *you* will too! It may not be exactly what you expect it will be, but it will be a time of making unforgettable memories (hopefully some good and probably some less than good) that last throughout your life. Just know that the first week or two of school will most likely be fun, exciting, intimidating, and scary. All of this is a part of transition from high school to the rest of your life.

CONNECT WITH CAMPUS MINISTRY

We've already talked about the hectic pace of the first few weeks of school. If you don't work hard to commit to a disciplined schedule early on, your calendar will begin to control you rather than you controlling it. This is especially true for your growth as a believer.

Four out of five Christians leave the church within the first year of college. Many factors contribute to this reality. One is a lack of discipline. So repeat this principle to yourself: *My walk requires work.* Putting out effort is critical to your spiritual growth, especially during your freshman year of college.

Getting connected with a campus ministry is essential for you. This will not happen on its own. It will require effort. Those students who seek out a campus ministry their first week will dramatically reduce their probability of walking away from church during their first year.

I got involved in a campus ministry my first week of school. I met people that first night who are still some of my closest friends. Also, in my freshman year, I started singing in a group sponsored by a ministry on our campus. Three of the guys I met in that group were in my wedding seven years later. Another in this group owns a production company that handles all of the media, Web, and print design for our ministry. And one of the guys, Mike, is my best friend. He and I talk almost every day. We vacation together. We do ministry together. We do life together. I love Proverbs 18:24 (NIV), which says, "A man of many companions may come to ruin, but there is a friend who sticks closer than a brother." I found this friend because I got involved in campus ministry.

Campus ministry surrounded me with people who, like me, understood the importance of being in community to maintain a walk with the Lord. Campus ministry didn't replace my responsibility to attend and serve at a local church. But it did give me a place to worship on campus while also surrounding me with people who helped to keep me accountable, not to mention people who have impacted my career, my family, and my life choices to this day.

I encourage you to take the lead on this before your first week of school. Talk with the admissions department about the various campus ministries. Find out when and where they meet. Make it a priority of yours to get involved the first week. I am sure you won't regret it!

MISSING HOME IS NORMAL

Leaving your family, friends, and everything you've known your entire life can be an emotional experience. If your family ever moved while you were still living at home, you have a good idea of what it's like to be thrown into an unfamiliar environment. The good news is, most freshmen on campus are dealing with the same emotions you are.

I missed everything about my home the first few months of school—my family, my dog, my bed, and even my own toilet!

Though it may be difficult at first, try to focus on the excitement of this new season of your life, rather than focusing on what you miss back home. Call home, but try not to do so every day. If you live close enough to drive home on the weekends, try not to do this, at least for the first few weeks. As I stated in the relationship chapter, staying in communication with your family is important. But learning to maintain those relationships with restrictions will help to give you the time you need to adjust to your new environment without a constant emotional pull.

Time Management Is Essential

Gone are the days of Friday night football games, picking out the perfect prom dress, cruising the town with friends, playing on the Xbox until three in the morning, and senior skip days. Sure, the first semester of college will be a blast. But it will also be a bust if you do not learn the importance of time management, and learn it fast. There is a great warning for this in Proverbs 26:14-15 (NIV):

> As a door turns on its hinges,
> so a sluggard turns on his bed.
> The sluggard buries his hand in the dish;
> he is too lazy to bring it back to his mouth.

Look, there's no one there to get you out of bed for class after you hit the Snooze button for the fourth time. (Unless you have a roommate who is cool with that!) This is college. The real world. And the old saying has never been more true than when it comes to college life: If you snooze, you lose!

1. Manage the Distractions

You will learn quickly that at college there is almost always a party going on somewhere. Social life at school rarely sleeps.

It's important to make new friends. But it's just as important to manage time spent with these friends. This means that there will be times when you just have to say no. Don't allow the noise of the crowd to lure you into believing that you have to be the person who attends everything.

2. Manage Your Attendance

I'll never forget Christmas break of my freshman year. I was home with my family when the grades from my first semester arrived. You can imagine the look on my dad's face when he saw three D's! No, it didn't read "3-D"! I wasn't majoring in high-tech movie animation. I received three D's in school that semester. One was in Freshman English. (Remember, Ms. Williams?) One was in Accounting 101. One…was Men's Choir. (At that time, I was a music major.) Yes, choir!

Men's Choir was an 8:00 a.m. M-W-F class. Dean Ensminger was my professor. He made it clear to us men that all we had to do to make an A in his class was to show up and sing. He also made it clear that for every two classes we missed, our grade would drop one letter. I missed class six times that semester. I hope you'll learn now what I should I have learned then before choosing to sleep in on those days. It's amazing how six hours of sleep cost my GPA. It took me several semesters to correct the low start to my GPA.

Many professors won't say anything to you if you miss class. That's your choice. But if you miss, it's also your loss. Make 100-percent class attendance your goal. You'll find that if you don't manage your class attendance, it will be easy to rationalize sleeping in or skipping out on an evening class to hang with friends. Don't start a bad habit that you'll later regret. Trust me, it's no fun sitting around the family Christmas tree convincing your dad that Men's Choir was just too intense of a course to take your first semester!

3. Manage Your Study Time

I wish someone had told me how much study time would be required of me to make the grade in college. As a general rule, two hours of study time will be required for every hour you are in class your freshman year. If you are taking fifteen hours of courses, plan on forty-five hours a week for studying. As you can see, getting behind one week makes it difficult to catch up. And if you are accustomed to a teacher posting homework assignments online in case you miss a class, wake up! This is college.

4. Manage Your Room

One great thing about moving out of the house and into a dorm is that no one is there to make you clean your room anymore. One bad thing about moving out of the house and into a dorm is that no one is there make you clean your room anymore.

Sure, you can choose to let your dirty jeans lie on the floor until the dust bunnies carry them away. But this is now your home. And it should go without saying that keeping your room habitable is a good thing.

LIVE BY THE SYLLABUS

Your professors will most likely give you a class syllabus the first day of class. Your treatment of the class syllabus should be like the equivalent of cheese and pizza, Linus and his blanket, Batman and his mask.... In short, live by it!

Some professors will take the time in class to walk through the syllabus with you. Others won't. Either way, it's your responsibility to

Top 10 Thoughts of a Professor

10. If you are not in class, you aren't interested in passing this course.

9. Be professional, respectful, and considerate in my room.

8. This isn't the Student Center. Don't eat in my class.

7. If your eyes are closed while I'm talking, you'd better be praying!

6. If you arrive at my class late, you are rude.

5. If you leave my class early, you are rude and walking on thin ice with me.

4. A cell phone in my class...seriously?

3. If you are talking while I am talking, one of us had better stop. Guess who?

2. Do not work on other courses while in my class.

1. Nothing is more important than my class!

make sure you understand all that will be required of you in a class. Your syllabus will typically include course objectives, professor expectations, deadlines for papers and projects, test and quiz dates, reading schedule, how your class grade is calculated (that is, tests, quizzes, projects, and papers), and attendance expectations.

You will find out quickly that most if not all of your professors are not really concerned about whether you come to class, turn in your projects, or study for tests. It's not their job to take your hand and walk with you through college. It's also not their responsibility to see that you pass their course; it's their responsibility to provide you the opportunity. And the syllabus shows you the way.

I've included a class syllabus that can be downloaded from our website at www.thegraduatehandbook.com, to give you an idea of what it's all about. Check it out and get used to what a syllabus will mean to you in college.

Take Advantage of School Resources

Many college freshmen enter their first semester assuming they already know how to study. I did. I graduated from high school with a 3.8 GPA. There were times in high school that were academically challenging for me but none that were super intense. But I found out fast that the study skills required to succeed in college were vastly different from those in high school. Many colleges will provide workshops that will help you prepare and give you practical training to help you understand the study, writing, and test-taking skills necessary. A tutor or study group is also an option.

In College, Be Prepared To:
1. Sit
You should try to sit at the front of the classroom. As silly as this may sound, sitting at the front of the classroom does two things for you. First, it keeps you near your professor. The more you

connect with your professor, the more your professor sees you are serious about the course. Second, the closer you are to the front of the room, the more likely you are to stay focused on the main thing rather than be distracted by others.

2. Read

If in the past you have not had to read much in school, your first semester of college will change all of that. In fact, it's going to happen the very first week!

3. Write

You will write—a lot. Don't buy the lie that you don't need to write down what you're hearing in class or reading for assignments. The amount of information that you will be expected to retain can be overwhelming, especially if you do not make a record of it. Take as many notes as you can every time you are in class. Use a laptop or iPad to ensure you make a digital copy. Know that you will probably be working on several papers and projects at a time. Figure out a strategy to write and store vital information that you will use throughout each semester.

KNOW YOUR ACADEMIC ADVISOR

Deciding what courses are necessary for you, particularly when you are undecided about your major, can be confusing. Work early in your first semester to develop a relationship with your academic advisor. He or she is there to help you make important decisions about classes and ultimately will play a vital role in helping you achieve your academic goals. Know the hours that your academic advisor is in the office. Ask him or her what is the best way to communicate, whether by making an appointment, writing an e-mail, or whatever.

Most executives in the business world have gatekeepers to weed out calls that don't require the attention of the executive. In the same manner, many academic advisors are the gatekeepers to em-

> Remember, you can't control anything or anyone other than you. You are only responsible for you.

ployers who are on the hunt for summer interns or are searching graduates for job prospects. Maintaining a strong relationship with your academic advisor can provide you with attractive internships and job offers that may not otherwise come your way.

You for You

College life will afford you many new and exciting privileges. Enjoy, have fun, and make amazing memories. But with this new season of privilege comes responsibility and an entirely new set of challenges. Know now that your goal shouldn't be to do it all right. You won't. And even if you get close to perfection, the unknown variables of new friends, a new boss, new professors, and a new home may throw you an unexpected curve ball.

Remember, you can't control anything or anyone other than you. You are only responsible for you. Colossians 3:23-24 (MSG) says,

> Don't just do the minimum that will get you by. Do your best. Work from the heart for your real Master, for God, confident that you'll get paid in full when you come into your inheritance. Keep in mind always that the ultimate Master you're serving is Christ. The sullen servant who does shoddy work will be held responsible. Being a follower of Jesus doesn't cover up bad work.

There are many who would love the privilege being afforded you to go to college. Use your privilege wisely, giving it your all for God. And, as Colossians reads, be confident that you will be rewarded.

Dear God,
I thank You for the privilege of going to college and furthering my
education. I ask that You protect me from the Enemy while I am
here. Bring me under the influence of professors and friends who
push me toward You, not away. I pray that while I am here at
school I will have opportunities to share Your name with others
and that You will use me to advance and grow Your kingdom. I
pray that when others see me, they see You in me. Amen.

Chapter 9

Principles of Success

Jeffrey Dean

What's your definition of success? If you don't have one, it's okay right now. And even when you think you do have one, it will probably be re-defined over and again throughout your life. Success is often measured differently from one person to the next. My reason for including this chapter in the *Handbook* isn't to help you define success. Rather, it is to help you as you begin the journey toward success.

In my own life, I have learned that true success isn't about financial gain or worldly accolades. Instead, it is about me becoming a better me, the *me* God is daily shaping me into as I encounter and experience life's celebrations and challenges. So in this chapter I give you the Top 10 Principles of Success that I am still learning (and probably always will be throughout my life). As you read each, I hope you will commit to a life of applying these principles as God daily shapes you into the person He knows you can be.

1. DON'T SET OFF THE LIE DETECTORS (BE TRUSTWORTHY)

During the last half of the seventh century b.c., the prophet Jeremiah was commissioned by God to warn His people of their lack of respect and outright defiance of His holy Word. The people of Jerusalem had turned to their own selfish ways and pleasures and were refusing to return to God. In Jeremiah 5:1 (MSG), God says,

> Patrol Jerusalem's streets.
> Look around. Take note.

Search the market squares.
See if you can find one man, one woman,
A single soul who does what is right
and tries to live a true life.
I want to forgive that person.

Obviously the phrase "one man, one woman, a single soul" is a hyperbole—an exaggeration to make a point. Jeremiah himself would have been such a person who tried to do right. But the intention of God here is to make the point that He longs to bless those who live upright lives.

Trustworthiness is a critical principle for your success. People want to place their faith, support, and finances in those who prove themselves honorable and trustworthy. I found this out the hard way my senior year

Trustworthiness is a critical principle for your success. People want to place their faith, support, and finances in those who prove themselves honorable and trustworthy.

of high school. I don't remember telling a lie to a friend of mine that year, but I do remember my friend adamantly believing that I did. Either way, she never got over it. During our Senior Banquet, while reading the senior predictions, she made this prediction about me: "Jeffrey will one day own his own business. The business: lie detector machines. Unfortunately, he will never become successful because every time he walks into his own factory, all of the machines will go off!"

Pretty cold, huh? These probably weren't her exact words. Nonetheless, I've never forgotten the gist of what she said. She thought I had lied to her. Therefore, in her eyes, I could not be trusted.

I learned a valuable (and embarrassing) lesson that day: no one likes a liar. As a matter of fact, Proverbs 12:22 (NIV) says, "The LORD detests lying lips." *Detests*. That's some pretty strong language from God—language you and I can't ignore. Ever since that incident in high school, I've worked hard to be a man of integrity who both sticks to what I say I will do and strives to always do what is right.

Throughout Scripture, especially in Proverbs, we see that God means serious business when it comes to being a person who is trustworthy:

> A good man obtains favor from the LORD,
> but the LORD condemns a crafty man. (Proverbs 12:2, NIV)

> The truly righteous man attains life,
> but he who pursues evil goes to his death.
> The LORD detests men of perverse heart,
> but he delights in those whose ways are blameless.
> (Proverbs 11:19-20, NIV)

> The LORD abhors dishonest scales,
> but accurate weights are his delight....
> The integrity of the upright guides them,
> but the unfaithful are destroyed by their duplicity.
> (Proverbs 11:1, 3, NIV)

George Washington once wrote, "I hope I shall always have firmness and virtue enough to maintain, what I consider the most enviable of all titles, the character of an honest man."

Learn now the importance of being a man or woman who can be trusted. Work hard to apply these principles to your life:

- If you don't believe it and don't mean it, don't say it.
- Don't mislead others with crafty statements or lying exaggerations.
- Make sure your yes is yes and your no is no.
- Be on time to meetings, classes, and events. Your consideration of others' time speaks volumes about your character.
- Just because you can get away with something doesn't make it okay. Remember, what you do in private will eventually shape how you live in public.

2. GIVE SOME TIME (VOLUNTEER)

You don't have to be perfect or famous to make a difference. Volunteering is a great way to impact the life of others. It's easy to say, "Why doesn't someone do something about that?" instead of being someone who actually gets things done.

You don't have to be perfect or famous to make a difference. Volunteering is a great way to impact the life of others. It's easy to say, "Why doesn't someone do something about that?!" instead of being someone who actually gets things done. Applying this principle of success will make you feel just as good as those receiving it. You can volunteer:

- in schools by helping mentor and tutor younger students
- by contributing toward environmental management, such as removing weeds or protecting endangered animals
- by helping to rebuild lives and communities following a natural disaster
- in politics by supporting a candidate or project
- at a hospital, senior citizens center, church, group home, Boys & Girls Club, homeless shelter, community center, and more!

There are countless ways you can volunteer. Find something important to you—something you are passionate about—and give some time to make a difference in the world.

3. NEVER CUT ANOTHER IN HALF (MASTER CONFLICT RESOLUTION)

A remarkable story of how King Solomon used great wisdom to resolve a conflict is recorded in 1 Kings. Two women came to the king, both claiming to be the mother of the same child. Since the two could not find common ground in the matter, the king said,

> "Divide the living child in two, and give half to the one and half to the other." Then the woman whose son was alive said to the king, because her heart yearned for her son, "Oh, my lord, give her the living child, and by no means put him to death." But the other said, "He shall be neither mine nor yours; divide him." Then the king answered and said, "Give the living child to the first woman, and by no means put him to death; she is his mother." And all Israel heard of the judgment that the king had rendered, and they stood in awe of the king, because they perceived that the wisdom of God was in him to do justice. (1 Kings 3:25-28, ESV)

Solomon proved that, although conflict can't always be avoided, it can be confronted in the right way.

Conflict is inevitable. Encountering conflicts won't be a question of *if* for you. Rather, of *when*. First, it is important to remember that relationships are important to God. (This is why I talked about this in detail in Chapter 3, "What Do I Believe About Relationships?") His desire is for you to have healthy relationships at home, with friends, in the workplace, and more. He wants you to thrive in your relationships no matter how difficult the situation. Second, when facing a conflict, rather than running from it, God expects that you handle it wisely, just as Solomon did.

Recently, a teen girl from Texas called my radio show to talk with me about her mom and sister. Her name was Rachel and she explained that several years ago she had started going to church and eventually gave her life to Jesus. Her mom and sister were not Christians, and she talked candidly with me about how their differing beliefs had caused dissension in their relationship. I could hear in her voice how sad she was that she and her family had grown apart.

She said, "Our religious and political views are so different that it's now hard for me to see things as they do and vice versa. I've even tried to avoid them in an effort to avoid fighting. Often, when we do talk, it just turns into a verbal fight and nobody wins!"

I offered some possible solutions to help Rachel find commonality with her mom and sister rather than looking for ways to avoid them. This can be easier said than done, I know.

For conflict to be resolved, everyone involved must take ownership. Obviously, this is tricky because you cannot control what others do. And, in a case like Rachel's, it's hard to meet in the middle when your beliefs aren't aligned with others. But you can control what *you* do. Your job is to make sure that you are doing your part to make your relationships better, not worse. Sometimes this means you have to really think through what you say before saying it. Additionally, sometimes you have to be willing to choose *not* to speak and pursue peace, rather than continuing to speak (or scream) in an effort to simply win a war of words. Romans 12:18 (CEV) says to "do your best to live at peace with everyone."

How to Handle Conflict

1. Manage your emotions.
Stay calm when a conflict arises. Losing control of your words and actions can be costly. Saying something out of anger, even when you are right, could cost you a relationship, position, or career.

2. Be picky.
Choose your battles carefully. You may win the battle but lose the relationship in the process. Some fights just aren't worth the fight.

3. Separate the person from the problem.
You won't always agree with others about everything. And others won't always agree with your beliefs and convictions.

There may be valid reasons as to why someone sees something differently than you do. By looking past the person to the problem at hand, you can work to debate the issue without damaging the relationship.

4. Examine and explore.

Check out all the facts. Give each party involved the opportunity to clearly articulate his or her beliefs. Then explore options. Be open to the possibility of bringing another viewpoint into the conversation. If needed, take some time to step away and gather your thoughts before proceeding.

5. Forgive.

Conflict resolution is almost impossible if one or both parties can't forgive.

6. Forget.

Let the past be the past and work to make the future better.

4. CALL YOUR MEMAW (BE GRATEFUL)

If you can read this book, you should be grateful. Many people can't read at all. If you are able to walk, you should be grateful. Many people cannot walk. If you have someone to call friend, you should be grateful. Many people live lonely lives.

Being grateful is an important principle for your success. Many people aren't grateful. Watching the news on TV or reading the headlines on your favorite news site on the Web, it's easy to see that many people focus on the negative. Learning to express gratitude about your life and encouraging others about theirs will be an asset that others see in you.

People want to be around people who are grateful. People want to surround themselves with others who encourage them and have a positive outlook on life. Being grateful isn't something that comes naturally. I can admit that it is much more natural, and easier, for me to focus on what I don't have than on what I do. This is something I have to work at.

My grandmother, whom we call Memaw, has taught me a lot about being grateful simply by how she lives her life. She is now in her nineties. She still drives, swims, plays cards, and teaches Sunday school at her church. Regularly, I receive handwritten notes from her in which she talks about her friends, her health, and the beautiful flowers blooming outside. She has always encouraged me to be a better man, father, and husband. She has survived her parents, husband, son, granddaughter, and countless cousins and friends. She has watched friends and family members struggle with cancer, alcohol, drug addiction, and divorce. Yet I can honestly say that I cannot remember one time ever hearing my Memaw say something negative.

A few months ago, she had one of her toes removed. I called her after the surgery to ask how she was doing. She replied, "I'm great. Now I have one less toe to be concerned with!"

Be grateful for your life. Celebrate it every day. Here is a list of things you can do to express your gratitude:

- Be like my Memaw. Take the time to send a handwritten note to someone.
- Work to see the best in others.
- Say hi to someone you don't know.
- Let your boss know how thankful you are to have a job.
- Thank God for sending His Son, Jesus, to give His life for you.
- Call your Memaw to say "I love you" while she is still living.
- Text your dad and tell him how much you appreciate him.
- Text your mom too!
- Tweet the world and tell them how much you love life.

5. TAKE SPEECH CLASS (DEVELOP COMMUNICATION SKILLS)

To date, I have delivered messages in front of more than 3 million people. I have spoken in over two thousand public and private high schools. I have shared the stage with musicians and bands such as To- byMac, the Newsboys, Chris Tomlin, Third Day, Lincoln Brewster, MercyMe, Casting Crowns, and Jars of Clay. I have spoken to crowds of just about all sizes at conferences, churches, banquets, detention centers, and more, including a crowd of more than thirty thousand several years ago at Creation Music Festival in Pennsylvania.

Why am I sharing this information with you?

No, I am not bragging or name-dropping. I want you to know that for a long time I was scared to death of standing in front of crowds of people. That was, until Communication 101.

Communication 101 was a required class in my major at Belmont University. Most people got it out of the way during their freshman or sophomore year. Not me. I put it off until my senior year. I kept avoiding it, hoping somehow it would go away. But of course it never did. I heard horror stories from friends who had taken the class—stories of having to stand in front of more than thirty classmates delivering the required five different speeches throughout the semester; stories of sweaty palms, forgotten lines, and public humiliation. Before taking the class, I hated public speaking more than I hate flossing my teeth! (Does anybody love flossing?) But there was no escaping Communication 101.

I still remember the first speech I gave that semester. The professor let each student choose any topic he or she wanted. I chose my family. I talked about my parents, my brothers, and my life before college. It went better than I had thought it would. And by speech three, I re- ally felt comfortable in front of my classmates. I received an A in that class! Little did I know that this would be the beginning of the rest of my life.

I am so thankful that I was required to exercise my communica- tion muscles in college. Actually, I wish someone had pushed me ear- lier in life to overcome my fear of public speaking.

Developing your communication skills will be one of the greatest assets to your success. Whether you are standing in front of thousands or simply developing relationships among those with whom you come in contact in the workplace, your neighborhood, or elsewhere, your ability to clearly and confidently articulate your views will be priceless.

I encourage you to seek out opportunities to hone your communication skills. If college is in your forecast, my advice is that you take every class you can that will help you develop such skills. If you are not going to college, look for other opportunities, such as teaching a class at your church or mentoring kids in a Big Brothers or Big Sisters program. The more you work at developing your communication skills, the more confident you will become and the more credibility you will earn among friends, family, and co-workers.

6. LISTEN; DON'T JUST HEAR (LISTEN TO OTHERS)

Good communication begins with listening. So a lack of listening is one of the biggest obstacles to communication.

Know this: there is a difference between *hearing* and *listening*. You hear a lot of noises every day—music; countless conversations during lunch seemingly happening all at once in the cafeteria at school; your younger sibling banging on your bedroom door asking to borrow a shirt, your favorite shoes, eyeliner, money.... You get the idea. Most people hear fairly well. But few master the art of listening well.

James 1:19 (MSG) says, "Lead with your ears, follow up with your tongue." And Proverbs 1:5 (NIV) says, "Let the wise listen and add to their learning." Jumping to conclusions, displaying a lack of conviction, becoming distracted, losing patience, overreacting, and interrupting are all barriers to effective listening. Becoming a better listener isn't a simple process. But learning to listen is a critical principle you need to succeed.

Here are some steps to take to become a better listener:

- Be patient. When someone is talking, listen to everything the person says before responding.

- Listen to the story behind the message. Stories can help you connect with the person talking and enable you to better grasp the point being made.
- Confirm. When someone is telling you something, make clarifying summaries such as "So you are telling me…" or "I believe what you are saying is…"
- Encourage. Ask the one speaking to you to explain more. Look at the person and acknowledge that you are listening. Nod your head and use the person's name when responding.
- Take notes. After all, life is busy and there is much that competes for your attention. Note taking is like a backup for life's important moments that you can't afford to miss. The more notes you can take, the more prepared you are, especially if you are prone to forgetting things. Write down what the other person is saying. (This will be a useful habit for you in college and in the workplace.)

7. The Good Doesn't Always Feel Good (Receive Correction)

Here's some really good advice that a friend once gave me. (Warning: It won't sound good. But it is good.) Ready?

You aren't always right!

My friend was right. I'm not always right. And the same is true for all of us. No one is *always* right. Each of us gets it wrong about something at one point or another. And though it doesn't feel good to have someone tell you that you are wrong, it's essential that you understand that receiving correction is an important principle to your success.

Those who choose to accept this principle and apply change where it is needed are often better positioned to succeed. In case you are still questioning the need for such correction, there are three passages that should remove any doubt.

First, Galatians 6:1-3 (MSG) says, "If someone falls into sin, forgivingly restore him, saving your critical comments for yourself. *You* might be needing forgiveness before the day's out. Stoop down and reach out to those who are oppressed. Share their burdens, and so complete Christ's law. If you think you are too good for that, you are badly deceived." Galatians 6 therefore makes it clear that we are to receive correction when correction is needed.

Each of us gets it wrong about something at one point or another. And though it doesn't feel good to have someone tell you that you are wrong, it's essential that you understand that receiving correction is an important principle to your success.

Also, Proverbs 9:8-9 (HCSB) confirms the good that comes from the receiving of correction, saying, "Rebuke a wise man, and he will love you. Instruct a wise man, and he will be wiser still; teach a righteous man, and he will learn more." These two verses in Proverbs prove that if we are willing to receive correction, we will be all the wiser for it.

Last, in Proverbs 1:23 (HCSB), there is a promise from God to those who choose to hear, receive, and ultimately *apply* correction: "If you respond to my warning, then I will pour out my spirit on you and teach you my words."

8. WORK HARD AT EVERYTHING (BE DILIGENT)

The following verses sum up this principle of success:

The sluggard craves and gets nothing, but the desires of the diligent are fully satisfied. (Proverbs 13:4, NIV)

Poor is he who works with a negligent hand, but the hand of the diligent makes rich. (Proverbs 10:4, NASB)

Make every effort to be found spotless, blameless and at peace with [God]. (2 Peter 3:14, NIV)

The diligent find freedom in their work; the lazy are oppressed by work. (Proverbs 12:24, MSG)

He was diligent in every deed that he began in the service of God's temple, in the instruction and the commands, in order to seek his God, and he prospered. (2 Chronicles 31:21, HCSB)

As long as it is day, we must do the work of him who sent me. Night is coming, when no one can work. (John 9:4, NIV)

The one who stays on the job has food on the table; the witless chase whims and fancies. (Proverbs 12:11, MSG)

In short, work hard and God will bless you. Don't, and He won't!

9. DON'T FALL (BE HUMBLE)

Indian poet Rabindranath Tagore said, "We come nearest to the great, when we are great in humility."

Being humble isn't the easiest principle of success to master, especially when the cultural slogan of the day is "Get all you want, the way you want it, how you want it, and when you want. You deserve it!" Time and again, the Bible associates humility with wisdom and warns that the opposite of humility—pride—will lead to a great fall: "When pride comes, then comes disgrace, but with humility comes wisdom" (Proverbs 11:2, NIV).

I experienced such a fall—literally!

Several years after graduating from college, I recorded my first CD. (No, I really can't sing. I just thought I could back then.) Over the next six years, I lived the life of a musician. I hired a band. I recorded two more CDs and was making a living doing what I loved to do. I can still remember how incredible it felt to travel from city to city and hear my songs being played on the radio.

One night while in Florida, I played at a large youth event with several other bands. I was on right after a local band, which used a fog machine that filled the stage with a thick mist. It was the perfect concert environment: a packed house, an energetic crowd, and fog pouring off the stage into the audience with lights piercing through it. I remember thinking this would be a night I'd never forget. Well, I was right about that. I ran out on stage, grabbed my microphone, and fell right off the edge of the stage into the crowd. (You guessed it. Thick fog.) This wasn't your average stage. This was six-feet-off-the-ground staging. I guess you could say I did my first stage dive that night. Except when I dove—okay, *fell*—the crowd moved back and I went *splat*. I climbed onto the airplane the following morning a sore and humbled man.

Up until that I point, I was a pretty prideful guy. I thought I was all that. I was chasing *my* dream to play music, rather than humbling myself to listen to the voice of God and hear what He had for me. I now understand better the pain in the *fall* that Proverbs 18:12 (NIV) warns of. "Before his downfall a man's heart is proud, but humility comes before honor."

God wants you to develop a character of humility. Colossians 3:12 (NIV) says, "As God's chosen people, holy and dearly loved, clothe yourselves with compassion, kindness, humility, gentleness and patience." Humility is all about putting God and others before yourself. Philippians 2:3 (NIV) says, "Do nothing out of selfish ambition or vain conceit, but in humility consider others better than yourselves." So avoid the fall, work to put others first, and take my advice—stay off the six-feet staging!

10. DRIVE A CLASSIC (VALUE YOUR LIFE)

I had a candy-apple-red '66 Ford Mustang in high school. (If you are drooling right now, then you are either a fan of cars or you just really like apples.) I bought it for about $1,000. And then spent about another $3,000 and two years working odd jobs on nights and weekends cleaning offices, doing construction, bagging groceries, and even selling Christmas trees to make money to get it drivable. Many of my friends thought it was silly of me to put so much time and money into something so old. To them, it was just a car. To me, it was far more valuable than just a car. It was a classic, and I loved my 'Stang.

You may have something just as valuable to you. It's healthy to have things in life that motivate you to accomplish goals and dreams. But of all the things that you place a high value on, nothing should be greater than the value you place on living your life to honor God. He created you and has a remarkable plan for your life. He thinks a lot about you, and He wants you to think a lot about you too!

Matthew 10:29-31 (MSG) says, "What's the price of a pet canary? Some loose change, right? And God cares what happens to it even more than you do. He pays even greater attention to you, down to the last detail—even numbering the hairs on your head! So don't be intimidated by all this bully talk. You're worth more than a million canaries."

So how many hairs do *you* have on your head? It's almost impossible to know, isn't it? But God knows. He knows everything about you, even down to the last hair on your head.

Why is this good to understand? Well, probably for many reasons. But this is especially good news for you to hold on to when you are having one of those days when it feels like the world would be better off without you. If you haven't felt like this, hold on. You probably will at some point during the first five years of post-graduation. I know I did.

The truth is, we all have times in life when there are uncertainties. During these next few years of your life, there will be questions, struggles, disappointments, and fears. This is why it is so comforting to know that God understands this. He knows what you are about to face and He knows what you want and need more than you do. He knows what you're doing right now and what you will be doing five years from now.

God knows absolutely everything about you. And when He looks at you, He sees your beauty and your potential. God wants you to know He's on your side! Look what Psalm 139:13-16 (MSG) reveals what God knows about you:

> Oh yes, you shaped me first inside, then out;
> you formed me in my mother's womb.
> I thank you, High God—you're breathtaking!
> Body and soul, I am marvelously made!
> I worship in adoration—what a creation!
> You know me inside and out,
> you know every bone in my body;
> You know exactly how I was made, bit by bit,
> how I was sculpted from nothing into something.
> Like an open book, you watched me grow from conception to birth;
> all the stages of my life were spread out before you,
> The days of my life all prepared
> before I'd even lived one day.

Sounds to me like God is saying, "Hey, you are valuable to Me!" Remember this. Seriously! Remember what God says about you. God wants you to know that you were made for more—more than just getting by, settling, or giving in. Before you drew your first breath, God knew you. And ever since, He has had His hand on every aspect of your life. He knows you better than you know yourself, and He even knows the things you don't know about yourself—like the amount of hair on your head! So, in the years ahead, if you ever start to wonder if you're even "worth it," pause and remind yourself that the Creator of the universe knows a lot about a million canaries... and He knows even more about you!

Now take a moment and pray, thanking God for how He made you. The journey is just beginning. And the best days of your life are too!

Dear God,

I want to be everything You created me to be. Help me to apply principles to my life that honor You. Help me prove myself trustworthy and of character to my friends, family, and co-workers. Show me where and when to give of my time to help others and glorify You. Teach me how to deal with conflicts by not compromising Your Word. I want to work hard at all I do and delight You in all my ways. Thank You for my life and thank You for seeing me as a person of value. Amen.

Chapter 10

What Really Matters Most

Jeffrey Dean

If you are a sports enthusiast, then you can probably remember who won the last Super Bowl, NBA Championship, or World Series. If you are a gamer, then it probably doesn't take you long, with controller in hand, to attain high levels on your favorite game. Maybe music is your deal. If so, there is a good chance that a mix of lyrics from various artists is shuffling through your mind at any given time. Or maybe you are a meaningless trivia nut. If so, you may enjoy questions like these:

- Which ocean—the Pacific or the Atlantic—is saltier?
- What is America's favorite flavor of ice cream?
- True or false? Babies are born without kneecaps.
- What is the last name of Elmo from *Sesame Street*?
- Or my favorite meaningless trivia question: forty thousand Americans injure themselves each year using _____?

You probably have a few of your own really good meaningless trivia questions.

Whether it's sports, music, trivia, or something else, have you ever stopped to consider how much knowledge you possess? I am confident that we all know a lot about things that are important to us. I'm also confident that we all know a lot about things that really don't matter for eternity.

Answers to the trivia questions: Atlantic. Chocolate. True. Monster. The toilet. (Can't imagine or explain that last one.)

I've included this chapter in the handbook because I want to talk with you about four things you need to know about what really matters in your life. You see, having a wide range of knowledge is important, but equally as important is the *depth* of your knowledge. Consider this: It doesn't really matter what you know if you don't know what really matters. In many ways, these first seventeen or eighteen years of your life have been the training ground for what's next. God has a super big plan for what is next in your life—for what really matters! Let's talk about it.

I MATTER!

To God, everything about you matters—your goals, aspirations, weaknesses, challenges, desires, ambitions, choices, relationships, past, present, and future. It all matters to Him.

You are no accident. You are a person of significance and meaning. When God made you, He was really showing off. Look at what Colossians 1:16 (MSG) says about you, "Everything, absolutely everything, above and below, visible and invisible…—*everything* got started in him and finds its purpose in him." The key word here is "everything"! Everything excludes nothing. That means you are included in the *everything!*

To God, everything about you matters—your goals, aspirations, weaknesses, challenges, desires, ambitions, choices, relationships, past, present, and future. It all matters to Him.

Stacey, a senior in high school, approached me after I finished speaking at a Youth For Christ event recently to say, "I'm really freaked about next year. I know God has a plan for me, but I'm nervous about figuring it all out." I encouraged Stacey to really work at enjoying the ride during her senior year. I told her that the questions and uncertainties she has about the *what's next* after high school are a normal experience. And God wants to teach her to trust Him during all of this because she matters to Him.

You need to know this too! The ending of the high school years and the beginning of the rest of your life can be scary and intimidating. But know this: you do not face it alone. And no matter where you have been or what you have experienced, your past does not dictate your future with God. Psalm 139:16 (HCSB) says, "Your eyes saw me when I was formless; all my days were written in your book and planned before a single one of them began." This verse is proof that God will do what He desires to do with you. You have a purpose. It's a God-given purpose, and He wants to help you fulfill your purpose because you matter to Him.

I have seen in my own life that Satan often spins his web of lies during times of transition. Be ready! He will try to use this transitional period in your life to confuse and misguide you. He knows the next five years of your life are pivotal to the next many years, and he will work overtime trying to discourage you and convince you that you don't need to take God or His Word into the next chapter of your life.

Prayer must be an integral part of your life going forward. Pray for protection. Pray for focus. Pray, keep pursuing God's truths, and let Him remind you of His love, plan, and purpose.

TIME WITH GOD MATTERS!

Dear Jeffrey,

I'm seventeen and graduating from high school in a few months. I don't have a "horror stories" past. I really like my parents. I'm into my church. I've never had a drink or gone all the way with a girl. I guess you could say I do most things really well, and that's the truth. But what keeps grinding me is that I can't say I feel really close to God right now. I mean, I know Him and love Him, but I don't really feel like I'm connecting with Him. Help?

Thanks,
Mason

I have seen in my own life that Satan often spins his web of lies during times of transition. Be ready! He will try to use this transitional period in your life to confuse and misguide you. He knows the next four years of your life are pivotal to the next many years, and he will work overtime trying to discourage you and convince you that you don't need to take God or His Word into the next chapter of your life.

I hear this story a lot from teens. My response to Mason, and to *any* teen who shares a similar story, is always the same: "How much time are you spending with God in the Word and in prayer?" Think about this question. How much time can *you* say you have spent with God in the last year of your life? Are you satisfied with the amount of time that you give God each month? Each week? Each day? It could be that if you can relate to what Mason said about your connection to God, then you, too, need to take a look at the amount of time you're giving God each day. The more time you spend with Him, the more you get to know Him, His love, and His will for your life. It is impossible—let me say it again, *impossible*—to know and do God's will if you are not spending time with Him.

Where do you see yourself in five years? Where will you be working? What kind of car will you drive? What city will you live in? Who will you marry? What house will you buy? What investments will you make? What church will you serve in? How will you use your finances to support a family, give to church and charities, and save for retirement? These questions are just a few of the many big ones you will be asking in the next five years of your life.

So, do you have all the answers now? No, of course you don't. But guess who does? God *could* choose to give you the answers to all of your big questions today. But what fun would there be in that? There'd be no adventure, no surprises, and for sure no need for God if you knew it all ahead of time. This is why time with God matters.

There are countless passages in Scripture that give us proof that spending time with God works. Look at Psalm 119:104-105 (HCSB): "I gain understanding from Your precepts; therefore I hate every false way. Your word is a lamp for my feet and a light on my path." Want to know the answers to the biggest questions about the rest of your life? A professor can't give you that. Neither can your parents, your friends, your dates, or even Wikipedia. But God's Word can. Psalm 119 makes it clear that by spending time in the Word you'll gain knowledge and understanding about what really matters most.

If you haven't made time with God a priority, don't give up. It's never too late to start doing what is right. The important thing is that you commit now

Remember this: the key to knowing God more is being intentional. And repetition plays an important role here. Not so much in your approach, but in being intentional about spending time each day with God.

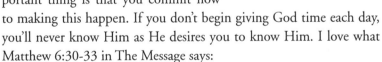

to making this happen. If you don't begin giving God time each day, you'll never know Him as He desires you to know Him. I love what Matthew 6:30-33 in The Message says:

If God gives such attention to the appearance of wildflowers—most of which are never even seen—don't you think he'll attend to you, take pride in you, do his best for you? What I'm trying to do here is to get you to relax, to not be so preoccupied with getting, so you can respond to God's giving. People who don't know God and the way he works fuss over these things, but you know both God and how he works. Steep your life in God-reality, God-initiative, God-provisions. Don't worry about missing out. You'll find all your everyday human concerns will be met.

In short, seek Him first. Giving God first priority in your life begins with giving Him your time.

With the potential of a new address, a new school, a new schedule, a new job, and new friends, your calendar may be a work in progress until you lock in your new rhythm. For a while, you may have to adjust your God-time each day. But the more you work to make a habit of it now, the more you will desire to spend time with Him.

Ways to Spend Time in the Word

There is no right or wrong way to be in the Word with God. Be creative:

- Try reading in different locations or reading various translations of the Bible.

- Get alone with God at different times of the day throughout the week. Mix it up until you discover what works for you, and then stick to it!

- Reading the same verse over will help you absorb the truth of Scripture.

- Find a quiet spot, unplug from the noise of your life, and just be still with God.

- Go to Starbucks or your favorite place and read your Bible and journal.

- Get with a friend or co-worker once a month to talk, read, and pray.

Read what one senior messaged to me on Facebook: "I've been getting into the Word more like you challenged us to at camp. You were so right! The more I'm in it (the Word), the more I get it. The more I get it, the more able I am to live it!"

Remember this: the key to knowing God more is being intentional. And repetition plays an important role here. Not so much in your approach, but in being intentional about spending time each day with God.

GIVING GOD MY ALL MATTERS!

You are probably familiar with the story Jesus tells in Matthew 25 of the man who gives talents (money of the day) to his servants before leaving on a journey. "To one he gave five talents, to another two talents, and to another one talent each according to his ability." Here's how the rest of the story goes:

> The man who had received the five talents went at once and put his money to work and gained five more. So also, the one with the two talents gained two more. But the man who had received the one talent went off, dug a hole in the ground and hid his master's money.
>
> After a long time the master of those servants returned and settled accounts with them. The man who had received the five talents brought the other five. "Master," he said, "you entrusted me with five talents. See, I have gained five more."
>
> His master replied, "Well done, good and faithful servant! You have been faithful with a few things; I will put you in charge of many things. Come and share your master's happiness!"
>
> The man with the two talents also came. "Master," he said, "you entrusted me with two talents; see, I have gained two more."
>
> His master replied, "Well done, good and faithful servant! You have been faithful with a few things; I will put you in charge of many things. Come and share your master's happiness!"

Then the man who had received the one talent came. "Master," he said, "I knew that you are a hard man, harvesting where you have not sown and gathering where you have not scattered seed. So I was afraid and went out and hid your talent in the ground. See, here is what belongs to you."

His master replied, "You wicked, lazy servant! So you knew that I harvest where I have not sown and gather where I have not scattered seed? Well then, you should have put my money on deposit with the bankers, so that when I returned I would have received it back with interest.

"Take the talent from him and give it to the one who has the ten talents. For everyone who has will be given more, and he will have an abundance. Whoever does not have, even what he has will be taken from him." (Matthew 25:15-29, NIV)

There are several things to learn about what it means to give God our all in this passage:

God Wants to Give You What You Don't Deserve

I can remember only one time while growing up that my grandfather, Pepa, punished me. I probably was seven or eight years old at the time. My older brother, Kent, and I were spending the week at my grandparents' house. I don't remember everything about the fight I had with my brother that day, but I do remember it had something to do with a chocolate chip cookie. I also remember my grandfather stepping in and, shortly thereafter, both of us being sent to different bedrooms to cool down and think about how ridiculous the two of us were acting over a cookie. After a while, I also remember my Pepa inviting us onto the back porch with him for a post-fight cookie and some milk. Obviously, neither of us deserved that cookie. But Pepa filled our tummies anyway! He did it because he loved us. Though he may have never fully known it, Pepa blessed Kent and me that day. And after all these years, I haven't forgotten that moment.

The man in Matthew 25 didn't have to give his servants anything. They were beneath him. But he did because he wanted to bless them. The same is true with God. He doesn't owe you or me anything! But He does want you to be blessed.

There is a misconception permeating culture today—it's called entitlement. Many believe that they deserve anything and everything they want. Many believe, "I should get what I want, because I deserve it!" Many people believe that they deserve *anything* they want, the *way* they want it, and at the *time* they want it.

The truth is, the only thing you and I deserve as sinners is hell! We don't deserve anything good. But God loves us so much that He wants us to get what we don't deserve.

Know that God desires to bless you and give you His very best.

God Wants to Use You Uniquely

The man in this story (representing God) gives each servant a talent *according to his ability.* He didn't give the same to all, because all people aren't the same.

God has blessed you with certain abilities and talents that are only for you. He hasn't made you like anyone else. You are unique. And God has something for you to do that no one else can do better than you. Your responsibility isn't to compare what you look like, who you are, where you live, how much you make, or what you accomplish in life with anything or anyone else.

There potentially will be the voices of many in your life in the next five years comparing you to others. Don't allow the comparison game to take you down the road of perceived inadequacy. You will never be like anyone else, because God made you to only be you.

God Wants to Teach You to Work Wisely

Have you asked God to show you what career He would have for you? He will if you ask Him. He may not reveal this to you right away. But in His way and in His time, God will make clear to you what His plans for you are. In the meantime, whatever is before you each day—whether it be a part-time job, fifteen-hour semesters in college, or volunteering in your community—God expects you to work wisely in all you do.

The man in this parable expected the same from his servants. He left town expecting them to take care of what he had entrusted to them.

Are you one who daily strives to take care of what has been entrusted to you? For example, one day you may be entrusted with being a stay-at-home mom. Of course, such a responsibility looks different than a calling other women you know may have in corporate America. But if it is your calling, God expects you do it wholeheartedly for His glory.

God Wants You to Do Your Part

Second Thessalonians 3:10-13 (msg) says,

> Don't you remember the rule we had when we lived with you? "If you don't work, you don't eat." And now we're getting reports that a bunch of lazy good-for-nothings are taking advantage of you. This must not be tolerated. We command them to get to work immediately—no excuses, no arguments—and earn their own keep. Friends, don't slack off in doing your duty.

Obviously, the man in this story had expectations for all three of his servants. It goes without saying that he wasn't thrilled with the news from the third servant. The third servant did nothing with what had been given to him. Fear, laziness, and apathy probably played a part in his choice to sit idle rather than work hard for his master. The result: the one who did nothing got nothing.

God expects you to work hard in all that you do to use the gifts He has given you for His glory. Colossians 3:17 (niv) says, "Whatever you do, whether in word or deed, do it all in the name of the Lord Jesus, giving thanks to God the Father through him." In school, at work, with your relationships, when everyone is looking and when no one is looking, God's expectations of you are always the same—give it all you've got!

God Doesn't Require That You Have All the Answers

The master never told his servants when, or even if, he would return. They had no idea what the future held or whether their jobs would continue. I can imagine that there were tempting moments, wondering when their master would return, wondering if he were even still living, and wondering how they would be provided for if something ever happened to him. We don't know how long he was gone. But Scripture tells us he was away for a long time. I imagine it wasn't easy on the servants waking up every day to the unknown. But it wasn't up to them to know the entirety of the story. Their only responsibility was to take care of what had been entrusted to them in that moment.

It is impossible to know all that lies ahead for you in life. And there will be moments in your life when it seems there are no immediate answers to the questions you have about school, finances, marriage, a career, and more. This is where trust in God will be critical.

Throughout Scripture we read time and again stories where God's people had to learn to trust Him. I wish someone had told me when I was graduating this important truth: You can't trust in the moment, the situation, or simply your feelings. But you can always trust that God has your best interest at heart, and He will never leave you!

God Wants to Reward Your Strong Work Ethic

"Take the talent from him and give it to the one who has the ten talents," says Matthew 25:28-29 (NIV). "For everyone who has will be given more, and he will have an abundance." The master rewarded the efforts of the first servant. He celebrated his accomplishments by giving him even more!

Ecclesiastes 2:24 (NIV) says, "A man can do nothing better than to eat and drink and find satisfaction in his work. This too, I see, is from the hand of God." When you give God your all, He honors you and He gives you satisfaction. So plan, strategize, work, and commit to God all you do. Proverbs 16:3 (NIV) says, "Commit to the LORD whatever you do, and your plans will succeed."

My Go Matters!

Just think for a moment about all the great things that have happened in your life. Don't even stop for a moment and try to say that your life isn't great. You are alive. You are graduating high school. And you probably have some really cool stuff that makes life really fun for you, like your phone, your laptop, or any number of digital devices you may own that connect you with friends, the Web, and the world. But the greatest one of all is the fact that, if you have given your life to Jesus, you are saved from hell!

The greatest part of the story of you is that God has created you, He has greatness in store for you, and He wants to give you the abundant life (John 10:10). What a privilege it is to know God and to know He loves you! Equally, what a privilege it is to share that love with another who doesn't know Him as Savior! It's what you are called to do you.

Sure, there may be an occupation God leads you to that is not defined (by the world's standards) as an occupation in ministry. But as a Christfollower, your number-one job is to share Jesus with the world. Every day is a life of ministry for you. This was the heartbeat of Jesus while He was on earth. Take a look at the first commission Jesus gave to those who would follow Him:

> As He was passing along by the Sea of Galilee, He saw Simon and Andrew, Simon's brother. They were casting a net into the sea, since they were fishermen. "Follow Me," Jesus told them, "and I will make you fish for people!" (Mark 1:16-17, HCSB)

Now take a look at the last commission of Jesus to all Christ followers:

> Jesus came near and said to them, "All authority has been given to me in heaven and on earth. Go, therefore, and make disciples of all nations, baptizing them in the name of the Father and of the Son and of the Holy Spirit, teaching them to observe

everything I have commanded you. And remember, I am with you always, to the end of the age." (Matthew 28:18-20, HCSB)

Do you see the resemblance in these two commands from Jesus? These are the first and last recorded commissions of Jesus in the Bible. I can summarize these two passages in one word. Jesus commissioned these men (and all Christ followers) to *go!*

Obviously, evangelism was pretty important to Jesus. And it's got to be important to us as Christians too.

You probably know someone who is not a Christian. I do. I have two neighbors, neither of whom are Christians. I see them frequently. They both know that my wife, children, and I are Christians. And I believe with all my heart that God has placed us in our neighborhood in part so that we can point them to Christ. We've had some really interesting conversations about God, and I know God has given me and my family a unique opportunity to live a God-honoring life in front of them. They haven't yet given their lives to Him. But I am hopeful that they will come to the place of surrendering it all to Jesus one day.

After high school, you will meet people all the time who do not know Jesus as Savior. It is very possible you will interact with them in various ways, such as working with them, sharing a dorm room with them, or maybe living next to them. Satan wants you to feel the *fear* when it comes to sharing Jesus with people you know and meet. God wants you to experience the *fabulous!*

There's no greater privilege in life than sharing the saving message of Jesus with someone else. Sometimes talking to a person about Jesus may seem impossible. But make no mistake, when God calls you to do something, He'll *never* require something of you that's impossible and He'll *never* require something of you that you have to face alone. First Corinthians 1:25 (CEV) says, "Even when God is weak, he is stronger than everyone else." Even in God's weakness (which He has none, by the way), He's still stronger than the greatest human strength. When talking with someone about Jesus, remember you're not alone. When God asks, He provides the way, the words, the courage, and the outcome. And know this too: the life you live speaks much louder than the words you say. Sharing Jesus with others will be an opportunity (and a privilege) you have every day. And, many times, this will happen without your even opening your mouth.

As you begin to settle into your new role as a graduate, I encourage you to begin praying like never before that God will give you His eyes, His ears, and His heart to see the world around you as He sees it—a world desperate for hope, love, and Him! Pray that you will see your interactions with people as opportunities to share Jesus. Pray that you'll then start to grasp the urgency before you like never before to be a voice of truth and light in a world seemingly running from both. Pray that your aspiration won't simply be to just gain knowledge. Rather, pray that God will teach you more and more the importance of knowing what really matters...to go!

Dear God,
Thank You for my life. Thank You for creating me with purpose. Thank You for loving me so much that You gave the life of Your only Son for me! Teach me each day how to give You all of me. Teach me to trust You, even when my feelings lead me otherwise. Thank You for all You've done for me so far in my life. Please lead me as I begin the next chapter of my life. I give it all to You! Amen.

Acknowledgments

From Jeffrey Dean:

To my wife, Amy—I love you.
To my girls—you are my joy.
Many thanks to Eric Stanford for an awesome edit.
Thank you, David Litwin, for your contribution to this book.
To graduating seniors—congratulations! May you become everything you desire and more. As you read this book, I pray you grow in wisdom and love for God and His Word, and that you learn to apply His truths to every aspect of your life.
To God be the glory.

From Robby McGee:

A special shout-out to all of the former graduates who sat in a classroom and allowed me to "practice" on them to help make this book a reality.

To Eric Stanford, thanks for pushing me during the edit...and re-edits!

To my son, Tyler, you are the best son a father could ever hope for and one of the greatest blessings in my life.

To my wife and best friend, Vanessa—your love for God, me, others, and life is truly inspiring. I love you much!

Thank You, God, for the special purpose and plan You have for me and everyone reading the pages of this book.

About the Authors

Jeffrey Dean is an ordained pastor, national communicator, author, and radio host. He is the founder of Jeffrey Dean Ministries, whose mission is "to equip people to know and grow in Christ more." A twenty-year veteran of teen and family ministry, Dean has risen to become an authority on teens and teen culture.

Jeffrey has spoken to more than three million people in churches, conferences, prisons, public and private schools, and music festivals. He has also partnered with such popular ministries as Youth for Christ, Back To The Bible, Fellowship of Christian Athletes, Josh McDowell Ministries, Teen Serve Ministry, and many local Boys and Girls Clubs and crisis pregnancy centers across the country.

A lover of writing, Jeffrey has a column in *Direction* magazine and is the writer of the multi-volume curriculum Flood, published by Serendipity House. His books include *Between the Lines: One-Liner Wisdom for Today's Guys,* and *Between the Lines: One-Liner Wisdom for Today's Girls,* published by Random House. In addition, he is the author of *This Is Me* and *Watch This* for teen girls and guys as well as *The Fight of Your Life* for parents.

Dean makes his home in Nashville, Tennessee, with his wife and their two daughters.

To learn more about him, go to jeffreydean.com or facebook.com/iamjeffreydean.

Robby McGee is an entrepreneur, writer, teacher, and musician. With more than twenty-five years of business experience, Robby currently serves as the CEO of an organization that funds mission projects worldwide through revenue generated from real estate holdings, market investments, business ventures, and donations.

On the music side, Robby is a former member of the band Mid South, which was nominated for a Grammy. His song "Without You I Haven't Got a Prayer" earned a Dove Award for country recorded song of the year. Robby also recently fulfilled one of his life dreams by recording his first piano instrumental project, *Reaching for Christmas*.

He and his wife, Vanessa, live in Tennessee and have a son, Tyler, who was Robby's initial inspiration for *The Graduate Handbook*.